Praise for
Take This Job and Leave It

"Terrific! Thorough and very clearly written."
—Dan Lacey, editor
Workplace Trends

"A manual which combines street-smart thinking, professional advice and insider tips."
—Peter Yessne, publisher
Staffing Industry Report

"Should be read by every mid- to upper-level executive interested in landing a new position."
—Nancy C. Schretter, publisher
The Search Bulletin

"Bill Radin knows what he's talking about...Headhunters have listened to him for years—now it's your turn!"
—Martin Yate, author
Knock 'em Dead series

Take This Job and Leave It

How to Get Out of a Job You Hate and Into a Job You Love

By Bill Radin

CAREER PRESS
180 Fifth Avenue
P.O. Box 34
Hawthorne, NJ 07507
1-800-CAREER-1
201-427-0229 (Outside U.S.)
FAX: 201-427-2037

TAKE THIS JOB AND LEAVE IT

ISBN 1-56414-057-1, $12.95
Cover design by A Good Thing, Inc.
Printed by Bookmart Press

To order this title by mail, please include price as noted above, $2.50 handling per order, and $1.00 for each book ordered. Send to: Career Press, Inc., 180 Fifth Ave., P.O. Box 34, Hawthorne, NJ 07507

Or call Toll-free 1-800-CAREER-1 (Canada: 201-427-0229) to order using VISA or MasterCard, or for further information on books from Career Press.

Library of Congress Cataloging-in-Publication Data

Radin, Bill.
    Take this job and leave it : how to get out of a job you hate and into a job you love / by Bill Radin.
        p.   cm.
    Includes bibliographical references and index.
    ISBN 1-56414-057-1 : $12.95
    1. Job hunting. 2. Career changes. I. Title.
HF5382.7.R33 1993
650.14--dc20   93-9644
                                                              CIP

Acknowledgments

The author wishes to thank those who helped make this book possible, including his family; plus all the dedicated professionals in the employment industry who offered me their wisdom and encouragement: Martin Yate, Dan Lacey, Peter Yessne, Paul Hawkinson, Peter Leffkowitz, Danny Cahill, Terry Petra, Bob and Larry Cowan, Lou Scott, Ralph Schepens, Tim Moffitt, Michael Zatzick, Ron Farnham, Bill LaPerch, Loren Williams, Bonnie Krstolic, Joe Rimsky, Frank Ahaus, Alan Schonberg, Michael Schulman and Mike Boyer.

Also, thanks to Steve Wigginton, Nancy Schretter, Bob Snelling, Sanford Rose, Barb Kordis, Linda Krutzsch, Pete Lajoie, Bruce Duncan, David Lloyd, Dimos Striglis, David Donville, Jeff Hager, Ken Weybright, Craig Carrigan, Roger Quinn, Andy Jamieson, Joe Bioty, Jeff Livingston, Jim Vose, Craig Fowler, Neil Griffen; and all the candidates and client companies who have worked with me through the years.

Special thanks to Betsy Sheldon, Gretchen Fry, Oscar Collier, Phil Laut, Betsy Rushing, Suzanne Whitaker, Ed Felson, Rick Oseas, Lynn Sontag, Pat Kelly, Howard Roberts, Andy and Barbie York, Tom Hynes, Ron Boustead, Ruth Rivin, Chris Mather, Bill Moss, Chuck Wiedeman, Phyllis Stutler, Helen Misner, Carol and Ed Montgomery, Guy Huxel, John Murphy, Randi Lorber, the patient staff of Kinko's and Plasti-Koil; and the Groveton High School class of 1970.

Take This Job and Leave It is dedicated to my loving and supportive wife, Ruth.

Contents

Introduction

Overcoming the Fear of Change

It was spring of 1986 in Los Angeles, and I was trapped.

Not by the smog or the congestion, but by my job. I had worked like a fiend for over a year, and had reached a conspicuous level of achievement. But the fact was, I felt paralyzed by my career situation, and powerless to do anything about it.

I was well-liked, well-paid, and recognized by the company I worked for as an up-and-comer. I had a friendly boss, a private office and a solid base of reliable clients. And yet the fast track at the L.A. office left me cold.

Why? Because for all the goodies my job gave me, I felt unfulfilled on a gut level, deep beneath the superficial trappings of success.

I couldn't put my finger on what was wrong. All I knew was that I had to make a change, and the sooner the better.

Perhaps you're in a similar situation. You have a job that looks great on the surface, but leaves you feeling drained and frustrated at the end of each day. You spend most of your work week wishing it were Friday, and your weekends praying that Monday will never come.

Not that you don't enjoy your current occupation. You do. You just wish you were working somewhere else, and you'd like some help in making the switch.

I was fortunate. I had a *lot* of help. In fact, I had been learning first-hand the "insider" techniques of successful job changing from the moment I began my career.

That's because I'm a headhunter—my job is to counsel other professionals contemplating a career move.

As a result of my specialized training and on-the-job experiences, I knew exactly how to evaluate personal and professional needs. I knew how to identify and target prospective employers, construct a dynamite resume, interview effectively, get an acceptable offer, and make a smooth transition to a new company. I just never had the occasion to use the techniques I'd learned for myself.

At first I was apprehensive about making a change—but the alternative was simply too hard to bear. After weeks of brooding, I decided I had no choice but to take control of my situation and implement the same job-changing methods that had helped so many others.

Looking back, I'm glad I changed jobs. Not only was I able to increase my salary (which more than *tripled* within three years), my new work environment helped me refine my professional and managerial skills in a way that's proven invaluable to this day.

But best of all, the change made a positive impact on my self-esteem, because my activities and surroundings became consistent with my personal values. In short, changing jobs was the right thing to do.

A unique perspective

I've spent the better part of a decade counseling hundreds of job changers, preparing them to deal with the complexities and emotional minefields of a competitive and often *confusing* job market. And now I'd like to share with you the secrets I've learned.

Headhunting has given me the opportunity to view the job changing process from a unique perspective. In addition to the insights I've gained from closely listening to the aspirations of candidates, I've been privy to the most critical concerns of the decision-makers in my client companies. As a confidential participant in the hiring process, I've learned a great deal about how people tick—and about the functional realities of today's employment game.

In my role as a broker acting on behalf of two interested parties, I've put together some of the most satisfying job placements you can imagine; placements that have changed candidates' lives for the better, and helped my client companies grow and prosper.

Of course, my job isn't easy. Often, problems will put deals on hold for weeks or even months until all the bugs are worked out. And candidates, ever vulnerable to the effects of delays, will become moody, or indecisive.

But still, each year millions of people change jobs, either on their own or with the help of recruiters. They've taken the necessary steps to improve the quality of their lives by changing their surroundings, their associations and the application of their talents.

You, too, can get the job you want. All it takes is the desire to change, and the skill to master the process. And yet many people feel paralyzed, unable to take control of their careers.

The reality of change

Usually, the biggest roadblock is *fear*.

That's because a major life change involves risk. And most of us avoid taking risks because we fear we'll be worse off as a result.

To help you succeed, this book will allow you to *minimize* risk by giving you the practical tools needed to plan each move, and make the right decisions.

By applying the principles in **Take This Job and Leave It**, you'll gain the same sort of advantage I had when I made my first career move; and you'll profit from the experiences of hundreds of others I've assisted as they made their trek towards career growth and job satisfaction.

Best of all, you'll be able to pursue your new job in a way that's consistent with your own unique personality and set of values. That's because **Take This Job and Leave It** treats you as an honest, intelligent individual. You won't be coached on how to write a phony resume, or be force-fed a lot of trendy, scripted interview responses. The objective is to get you the job you want, based on your own merits.

Who should read this book

If you're contemplating a career move, don't worry, you're not alone.

According to a recent survey published by *U.S. News & World Report,* 63 percent of all employees feel personally dissatisfied with the type of work they do. As a result, one out of every 14 people in the United States this year will change jobs.

I'm not advocating that you clean out your desk the next time the copier jams; I just want to help you make the right career decisions. In fact, I regularly advise people to *stay where they are* whenever I feel a career move wouldn't clearly be in their best interest.

However, once you've decided to make a move, I want to help you manage the process, and give you the benefit of my experience.

If you're currently employed (or you're unemployed, and you have a reasonably good track record), this book is definitely for you. If you're contemplating a radical career change, or you're just entering the work force, the information contained in **Take This Job and Leave It** will help you, too, though you may want to supplement your reading with materials designed for your specific situation.

Finally, if you're happy where you are, you might want to make a few mental notes, since you never know when your situation might change.

The only way to ensure your own job security is to keep your options open and know your current value on the professional market. Remember, the best time to interview is when you're in a position of strength.

1 Job Satisfaction: It's Your Right!

You and I are lucky—we live in a world rich in possibilities. Besides being able to select from an unlimited variety of occupations, we also have the right to find happiness in our daily work.

Naturally, everyone has a different definition of *job satisfaction*. For example, the job that seems fine to you may not be of much interest to your best friend, and vice versa.

The fact that you live in a free society gives you the privilege to decide your own fate. You have as much power in determining where you work as you do in selecting a spouse, a home, a car or a pet. Your choice of jobs really depends on how much you want to shape your career, and how much effort you're willing to spend to make the necessary improvements in your life.

If you're considering a job change, it's probably for one of three reasons:

1. **Personal.** You want to change your relationships with others. For example, you may have discovered that you're incompatible with the people in your company. Perhaps they have different interests than you; or they communicate differently or have different educational backgrounds.

2. **Professional.** You've determined a need to advance your career. For example, you've found that you

15

won't reach your professional or technical goals at
your present company; or that your advancement is
being blocked by someone who's more senior or more
politically oriented; or that you're not getting the re-
cognition you deserve; or that you and your company
are growing in different directions; or that you're not
being challenged technically; or you're not being
given the skills you need to compete for employment
in the future. Or you've simply lost interest in your
assigned tasks.

3. **Situational.** Your dissatisfaction has nothing to do
with personal relationships or career development;
it's tied to a certain set of circumstances. Maybe
you're commuting too far from home each day, or
you're working too many hours, or you're under too
much stress; or you want to relocate to another city
(or stay where you are rather than be transferred).

Whatever your personal, professional, or situational reasons may be, you're motivated by the desire to improve your
level of job satisfaction and make a change.

A few years ago, when I packed up my bags and moved
from Los Angeles to Cincinnati, my decision had nothing to do
with my career or the people I was working with. My dissatisfaction was purely situational. I wanted to trade a high-stress,
long-commute, manic routine for a more livable, slower-paced
lifestyle. (And by making the change, I became a statistic in a
larger demographic trend.)

The complete job description

In order to translate your *needs* into *results,* let's begin by
evaluating your present position—it's the first step in any job
change.

You'd be surprised how many people are unclear about
what they actually do for a living, and the way their jobs make
them feel.

For example, whenever I interview a candidate, the first
thing I ask for is a complete job description.

"So tell me, Bonnie," I begin. "What is it that you do at your present company?"

"Gee, Bill, I thought I told you already. I'm a systems analyst."

"All right, fair enough," I reply. "But would you please describe to me in detail the following two things:

1. What are your daily activities? That is, how do you spend your time during a typical day?
2. What are the measurable results your company expects from these activities? In other words, how does your supervisor know when you're doing a good job?"

Often, I discover that people are hard-pressed to come up with solid answers about the specific nature of their work. They're not exactly sure about their job responsibilities, and their lack of focus results in stress or counter-productivity.

While a little bit of stress is natural in any job, a steady diet of it can destroy your incentive to work. In fact, a recent study indicates a direct correlation between a person's lack of *task clarity* and his or her level of job dissatisfaction.

Try this exercise: On a sheet of paper, write a complete, current job description in which you list your daily activities and their expected, measurable results. This exercise will not only help you clarify your *own* perception of your work; it'll be useful later on when you begin to construct a resume and communicate to *others* exactly what you've done.

The power of values

Once you've described all the facets of your job, the next step is to understand the relationship between what you *do* and the way you *feel.*

I use the term *values* to describe personal priorities; as a yardstick to help you:

- Understand what types of work-related activities you really *enjoy.*
- Determine which goals or accomplishments are important to you and give you a feeling of *satisfaction.*

- Evaluate whether your personal priorities are in balance, or *in harmony* with your job situation.

Remember in the introduction when I talked about a seemingly great job that left me feeling unfulfilled? I felt that way because my situation was *incongruent* (or "out of sync") with my own set of values, or what was important to me as a person. In other words, my job *satisfaction* had turned into job *obligation*. Once I made a change, however, my job situation became congruent, or in harmony with my unique, personal needs.

Although it's fairly simple to identify which daily tasks you really enjoy, the task of scrutinizing your personal priorities can be tricky. That's because there are often factors unrelated to your job that can come into play.

For example, Jim was a consumer electronics sales professional who told me he wanted to make a job change. He was servicing a local California territory when I approached him with the opportunity to work for one of my client companies.

On the surface, the new job seemed ideal. Not only was my client company a prestigious manufacturer of home audio equipment; it'd be offering a much higher salary than what Jim was currently earning. What's more, the position would represent a big promotion. If Jim were hired, he would become the national sales manager.

But there was a problem—which I was able to identify in Jim's discussion of values.

"Before you interview for this position, Jim, I'd like to ask you something," I said. "What do you consider to be important in your life? Do you have any special outside interests you'd like to tell me about?"

"Well, I started bodybuilding a couple of years ago, and I'm very excited about it," Jim said.

"I see. So how often do you work out at the gym?"

"Actually, I train every morning for two hours before work. It gets me pumped up before I make my sales calls."

"That sounds logical," I replied. "But what would happen if you were to take on a bigger territory, and had to travel? Wouldn't that cramp your style?" I asked.

"Hmmm," pondered Jim. "It certainly wouldn't be very practical to have to find a new gym in every city."

"Would that affect your willingness to change jobs, knowing you'd have to curtail your bodybuilding activities?"

"Well, I never thought about it that way. But yes, I guess my bodybuilding is too important to give up."

"So aren't you glad you aren't going to waste your time and energy interviewing with my client company?"

"Yeah," said Jim. Thanks for sparing me the aggravation."

Let's get specific

Clearly, a job requiring a lot of travel wouldn't make Jim happy.

That's why it's a good idea to know what your values are. A simple way to sort through them is to answer the following questions:

- What work-related activities do you most enjoy?

- What professional goals do you most want to achieve? (And why are they meaningful?)

- What ethical, family, spiritual, personal, environmental and lifestyle considerations are important to you?

- Which of the above values are being satisfied in your current job? Which are not?

To demonstrate the importance of values in our decision-making process, consider the following:

- I witnessed a job-seeker turn down a position because he was an amateur athlete and he didn't like the air quality where my client company was located.

- Not long ago, I placed a candidate who was a long-distance runner. He took the position largely because his new boss was also a runner, and would understand his need to take off work twice a year to run the New York City and Boston marathons.

19

- I arranged for an engineer to take a job with a company that offered him a *demotion,* since being highly visible within his current employer's department made him feel uncomfortable.
- I helped a radar engineer change to a lower-paying job. The reason? The engineer was a member of the 1988 Olympic rowing team, and the new company was near a river.
- I once found an excellent job for a chemist who was also an avid taxidermist. At the last minute, the chemist turned down the job, which would have required his relocation from Utah to northern California. The chemist explained that the climate in California was unsuitable for stuffing ducks.

  Later, I discovered the duck-stuffer's true reason for turning down the new job. He had a hometown mistress, and he couldn't convince her to relocate to California with him.

The point is, we all have highly personal motivations which guide our career choices.

Gathering evidence

The ability to communicate what's truly important requires a skill that is more difficult to master than it may first appear. To illustrate, take a look at some of these commonly used expressions, and ask yourself what they mean:

"I'm looking for a job that offers more *security.*"

"I wish there were more *management opportunities* here."

"My company doesn't give me the *resources* I need."

"Maybe a new job would give me more *challenge.*"

"What I want is a chance to *participate.*"

As a headhunter, I hear word patterns like these from candidates on a regular basis. Although the motivation behind them is sincere, the meaning is often cloudy, since the definition of a word or phrase may vary, depending on the individual or situation.

For example, "security" to one person may mean protection from a layoff; while to another, it might signify coverage by the company pension or health insurance plan. To a third, "security" could imply that a particular job function or reporting relationship is static, and will never change.

I interviewed a candidate once who described the *challenge* she was looking for in a job as the opportunity to play third base on her company softball team. To another candidate, *greater participation* referred to his interest in deciding which manager would sit atop the dunk-tank at the annual company picnic.

When candidates tell me they're looking for *more money*, my antennae always perk up. I've learned to immediately fire back, "How much money do you mean, exactly?" since the answer I get can range anywhere from a 2-percent increase to part ownership in the company.

To avoid ambiguity in your search for values, you can use a question-and-answer methodology psychologists call an *evidentiary procedure*. This technique will help sharpen your own self-awareness.

Let's say you want more responsibility than you're currently getting. That's fine, except the term *responsibility* by itself is too vague. To really pinpoint the values you need to satisfy, ask yourself these types of questions:

- Exactly how would I *define* responsibility?
- What *changes* would occur in my job if I were given more responsibility?
- How would I describe the *function* of someone I know who currently has the responsibility I'm seeking?
- If I were to get more responsibility, what would it *mean* to me, in terms of self-concept or self-esteem?
- What *feelings* (such as pride, power, control or self-respect) do I attach to greater responsibility?

21

- What *tangible benefits* are connected with having greater responsibility? Money? Title? Perks, such as a company car, a private office or a health club membership?

By forcing yourself to gather emotional evidence and express your thoughts precisely, you'll not only avoid wasting your time chasing the wrong job; you'll help others, such as recruiters or interviewers, understand your needs.

And as a result of the value-gathering process, you may end up adjusting your goals or aspirations. For example, will more "responsibility" actually make you happier in the long run? Perhaps not, after you've given yourself the chance to redefine the word.

There's no right or wrong when evaluating what's important to you. The only thing that matters in your job search is that you can accurately determine the way you feel, and make decisions accordingly.

Don't worry, you're not alone

Candidates aren't the only ones who need occasional help in communicating their thoughts. A few years ago, I had an experience that taught me the value of getting concrete evidence from employers, especially when they describe the people they'd like to hire.

I was working on a search assignment for a new client—a giant, multibillion-dollar oil company. The company principals kept telling me that they wanted to hire someone with a strong "work ethic."

Shortly after my first candidate interviewed with the company, I called Bart, the hiring manager, to debrief him.

I could tell from his tone of voice that Bart was quite annoyed. Yes, he said, the candidate had the right background, and, yes, he could do the job all right. But the company would never hire someone like him. He just didn't have the right *work ethic.*

"Wait a minute," I protested. "The candidate attended a college with a very tough academic program, and he's been promoted quickly at his current job, and he's got good references..."

"But didn't you interview him in person?" Bart interrupted.

"Well, no," I replied. "He lives pretty far from my office, and it just wasn't practical."

"Bill, from now on, I'm going to have to insist that you *personally* interview each and every candidate before you send him to me, to see that he has the right work ethic," Bart said. "You see, we'd *never* hire someone like him. He has a *beard!*"

The job description makeover

Now that you know how to clearly define your values, the next step is to describe the changes you'd like to make in your new job.

To illustrate, listen to the way Pat, Craig and Neil talk about their respective situations, and how they take their values into consideration:

Pat: "I want to have *more autonomy* where I work. That would mean having a flexible schedule, working different hours each day at my discretion, without having to ask permission. I'd be able to leave early on Thursdays to take my daughter to her acting class, and in return, I'd be willing to spend several hours working at home during the evening and on weekends.

With my personal computer, I'd have access by modem to the database in my department, and I'd be able to make a significant contribution to the workload, any time, day or night. Most importantly, I'd be evaluated solely on my performance, not by the number of hours I've punched on a clock."

Craig: "I'd prefer to work *closer to my home.* I didn't think the amount of time I spent commuting was very important when I joined the company two years ago, but now it really wears on me to sit for an hour a day in traffic. It's not only nerve-wracking to deal

23

with all the crazy people on the freeway; I could be using the commuting time to be with my family.

The reduction of stress would improve my attitude, and give me a higher quality of life. If I could find a job similar to what I have now within a few minutes of home, that would make me happy."

Neil: "I'm interested in my own *career advancement.* If I stay at this company too much longer, I'll work my-self into a corner technically and never achieve my potential. The people here are nice, but I don't share their 'lifer' mentality. Look at Ed, my boss. He's been here 17 years, and although he's a really solid en-gineer, he's not familiar with any of the latest ad-vancements in technology. He'd have a hard time finding another job in this market, and it worries me, knowing I might someday be in his situation.

Besides, I won't be promoted until Ed retires. So I'd better leave soon, while I'm still attractive to other companies. That would give me the salary in-crease I deserve and the opportunity to learn new skills with people who are upwardly mobile and ag-gressive like myself."

Now it's your turn. As any advocate of goal-setting will tell you, the more specifically you're able to communicate what you're looking for, the faster you'll be able to get what you want.

Naturally, you'll want to be realistic with your expecta-tions, and think like a grown-up when considering your gripes. I'll never forget Barry, an engineering candidate I interviewed a few years back, who came into my office with a suicidal look in his eyes.

"Bill, you've really got to help me," he moaned. "My job is ruining my life."

"Your situation sounds pretty serious," I replied in my most empathic tone. "How long have you felt this way?"

"Gosh, I don't know, but I've got to make a change. My per-sonal life is awful."

"How do you mean, Barry?" I asked.

"I mean I'm never at home, and don't have any time to spend with my wife and kids. My company makes me travel constantly."

"Well, I can see how that might make you feel torn between your work and your home life. What can I do to help you?"

"See if you can get me a job where I don't have to travel all the time. I just can't stand the separation from my family," he pleaded.

My heart went out to him. "Sure, Barry, anything to help. But first tell me something. Exactly how often is your company making you travel?"

"Oh, it's terrible," he cried. "They make me stay overnight in a hotel at least one night every three months!"

Your job-changing strategy

Someone recently asked me whether I helped people get "better" jobs—or jobs that made them happier.

My answer was that the two were the same.

Of course, if you were to look at your career from a purely *strategic* point of view, I could give you four good reasons why it makes sense to change jobs within the same or similar industry three times during your first 10 years of employment:

1. *Changing jobs gives you a broader base of experience.* After about three years, you've learned most of what you're going to know about how to do your job. Therefore, over a 10-year period, you gain more experience from "three times 90 percent" than "one times 100 percent."

2. *A more varied background creates a greater demand for your skills.* The depth of experience gained from having had multiple, diverse employers makes you more valuable to a larger number of employers. You're not only familiar with your current company's product, service, procedures, quality programs, inventory system and so forth; you bring with you the expertise you've gained from your prior employment with other companies.

3. *A job change results in an accelerated promotion cycle.* Each time you make a change, you bump up a notch on the promotion ladder. You jump, for example, from project engineer to *senior* project engineer; or national sales manager to vice president of sales and marketing.

4. *More responsibility leads to greater earning power.* A promotion is usually accompanied by a salary increase. And since you're being promoted faster, your salary grows at a quicker pace.

Many people view a job change as a way of promoting themselves to a better position. In most cases, I would agree.

However, you should always be sure your new job offers you the means to satisfy your values. While there's no denying the strategic virtues of selective job changing for the purpose of career leverage, you want to make sure the path you take will lead you where you really want to go.

For instance, I see no reason to make a job change for more money if it'll make you unhappy to the point of distraction. Not long ago, I placed a project engineer with a company that offered him a $47,000-a-year job. Later, he told me that the same day he agreed to go to work for my client, he'd turned down an offer of $83,200 with another company. The reason? The higher offer was for a consulting position with an aerospace company in Detroit—a job that would have taken him down a road he felt was a dead end.

To me, the "best" job is one in which your values are being satisfied most effectively. If career growth and advancement are your primary goals, and they're represented by how much you earn, then the job that pays the most money is the better job. Your responsibility when contemplating a change is to evaluate what's most important to you.

> *The more clearly you connect your values with your work, the greater the potential for job satisfaction.*

2 Controlling Your Mental State

Because your job is one of the most important aspects of your life, it's natural to experience all sorts of feelings throughout the job-changing process.

Hey, wait a minute! It's the inner voice of logic. *What do feelings have to do with it?*

Well, your mental state can affect performance. Besides, why do you think people change jobs in the first place, if not to feel better about their work?

I don't know. For more money?

We could all use more money. But money's only a part of the reason most people look at other opportunities.

So what about feelings? How can they affect performance?

Psychologists have known for years that there's a direct link between a person's emotional state and the way he or she behaves. That's what phenomena like "performance anxiety" and "killer instinct" are all about.

That makes sense.

Furthermore, your emotions can also affect the way you make decisions.

Really?

Sure. Let's suppose I wanted to change jobs. Here's how I might feel as my search evolves:

Monday: Darn it! My boss gave me a lousy review. *(Frustration)*

I work as hard as anyone else around here! *(Indignation)*

I'll show him! I'll get a job with another company. *(Revenge)*

But this may not be the right time to make a change. After all, I'm in the middle of a big project. *(Indecision)*

Who knows, maybe I'm not very marketable. *(Self-doubt)*

Tuesday: Cowabunga, dude! A headhunter just called to arrange a job interview with another company! *(Excitement)*

The headhunter was really nice. She said I had the perfect background for an outstanding opportunity! *(Pride, high self-esteem)*

But the interview is tomorrow morning and I don't have an updated resume. *(Panic)*

I hope they'll like me. *(Insecurity)*

But, hey, what have I got to lose? *(Nonchalance)*

Uh, oh. Maybe I could get fired for interviewing with a direct competitor. *(Paranoia)*

Wednesday: *(After the interview)* Hey! I really like this interviewer! And the new company looks pretty neat, too. *(Attraction)*

I must say, I handled myself like a real pro. *(Surprise)*

Interviewing for a job is a piece of cake. Maybe I'll call up some other companies and talk to them, too. *(Overconfidence)*

Gee, I wonder what they thought of me at the interview. *(Curiosity)*

What if they offer me the job? I still don't know very much about them. *(Anxiety)*

Well, anything's better than what I have now. *(Desperation)* My company doesn't even appreciate me. *(Self-pity)*

Hah! I'd like to see the looks on their faces when I resign! *(Scorn)*

Wait! What am I saying? I can't just walk away from them, not after all we've done together. *(Guilt, betrayal)*

How would they survive without me? *(False sense of importance)*

I have to admit, they've treated me pretty well over the years. *(Divided loyalty)*

I wouldn't even be surprised if they offered me more money to stay! *(Wishful thinking)*

Thursday: So why haven't I heard from the headhunter yet? *(Concern)*

She said she'd call me yesterday. *(Disappointment)*

They probably chose a candidate with more experience. *(Rejection)*

What if they don't make me an offer? *(Disenchantment)* I'll have to stay at this dump the rest of my life. *(Disgust)*

Oh, well. The whole thing was probably a waste of time, anyway. *(Bitterness)* Hmmm. A hot fudge sundae would sure taste good right now. *(Sugar dependency)*

Friday: Hooray! They want to see me again! *(Enthusiasm)*

But they were concerned by my lack of marketing experience. *(Inadequacy)*

Big deal! What's there to know about marketing? *(Defensiveness)*

I wonder if this is the right job for me? *(Confusion)* I think I'd better consult my astrologer...

Stop! I can't stand it! The voice of logic hollers. *Why would anyone put himself on a roller coaster ride like this?*

Because this roller coaster, as you call it, is a vehicle for change. And when you commit to making improvements in your life, you have to acknowledge the extra emotional work that's involved. That's just the price you pay.

The inner game of change

Fortunately, the reward for a successful job change is well worth the cost; and a beneficial byproduct is the valuable lesson you'll learn about the "inner game of change." In the inner game of change, you're forced to trade *short-term feelings* for *long-term satisfaction.*

We already know that your job change will arouse a variety of emotions, some of which might be uncomfortable. In addition, your decision to move on will probably hurt or disappoint some people at your current company—it's unavoidable.

Think of it this way: when you make a major change, it's like sailing a boat counter to the current; you'll be pulled by some pretty powerful forces as you cut across wind and water. But by taking control of the rudder, you'll be setting the course *you* want. And in the long haul, that's the best course to take, since you'll be satisfying your goals.

So long as your intentions are sincere, and you keep your goals in sight, you'll make the right decisions, even if they cause a little short-term pain.

Enjoy yourself—keep an even keel

Many people enjoy the process of change; they find it stimulating, challenging and rewarding, even though there might be some emotional ups and downs.

To keep an even keel, here are seven techniques that can help you get the most pleasure from your new pursuit:

1. **Periodically review your values**. Reaffirm the key role that personal and professional priorities play in your decision to make a change.
2. **Think about how empowered you feel**. Congratulate yourself. Very few people have the courage to make significant improvements in their lives.
3. **Visualize the positive aspects of your new job**. Fast-forward six months or a year from now. What will the change mean to your lifestyle and your relationships?
4. **Reduce or eliminate your exposure to the fears, prejudices, and conflicting interests of other people**. Discuss your goals and your intention to change jobs only with those who've demonstrated their own orientation toward achieving positive goals.
5. **Keep your job-search activities confidential**. Don't ask the advice of those with whom you work; otherwise, you may become the object of rumor or speculation.
6. **Try to learn something from each new experience**. Change is the best form of education. Can you apply what you've learned to a future situation?
7. **And above all, stay positive!** Fill your mind with as much motivational material as you can from reading books or listening to tapes, and look for mentors or role models as sources of inspiration.

The ability to control your mental state will be a key factor in your performance during each phase of the job-changing process.

A matter of life and death

Of course, any changes in your personal life will also influence the way you make decisions. For example, I once represented a very fine candidate named Stephanie, who was being courted by one of my clients.

After several weeks of interviewing, Stephanie was offered a job by the company as its quality assurance manager, an extremely important position paying $55,000 a year.

On the morning I called her to officially extend the offer, I could tell from her tone of voice that something was wrong.

"Bill, you really caught me at a bad time," she said.

"But Stephanie, you should be elated," I replied, trying to cheer her up. "You got the job you wanted at a terrific salary."

"I don't care; leave me alone."

"But you want the job, don't you?" I couldn't figure out what the problem was.

"Leave me alone," she said. "Call me tomorrow."

"I'd like to, but I told the company I'd let them know your answer. After all, you and I worked together for weeks to get you this offer."

"Well, that's too bad; they'll just have to wait," she sobbed. "My guinea pig died this morning, and I can't make a decision!"

The more you control your mental state, the greater your chances become for getting the job you want!

---

3 A Dynamite Resume: Passport to the Job You Want

In a perfect world, no one would need a resume.

The candidates most suited to a particular job would simply be summoned forth to interview, based on his or her reputation and word-of-mouth referral.

Employers would carefully make their hiring decisions based on the candidates' verbal account of past performance, without regard to any kind of written documentation.

And companies would grow and prosper, having selected only the best and brightest from a large pool of qualified talent.

OK. And now the reality:

- Employers are so inundated with resumes, it often takes weeks, or even months to sort through them all to identify the candidates they deem qualified.

- Despite the administrative headaches and delays caused by processing resumes, companies rely heavily on the resumes they receive to screen for potential candidates.

- Given the choice of two candidates of equal ability, hiring managers will always prefer to interview the one with the most artfully constructed and attractive resume.

- For that reason, candidates with superb qualifications are often overlooked.

- And companies end up hiring from a more shallow pool of talent; a pool made up of those candidates whose experience is represented by powerfully written, visually appealing resumes.

Of course, many of the best candidates also have the best resumes; and sometimes, highly qualified candidates manage to surface through word-of-mouth referral. In fact, the referral method is the one I use to present talented people to my client companies.

But unless you can afford to rely on your "reputation," or on the recommendation of a barracuda recruiter, you'll need more than the right qualifications to get the job you want—you'll need a dynamite resume.

In today's competitive employment market, your resume has to stand out in order to get the attention of the decision-maker and create a strong impression. And later on, when you meet the prospective employer face to face, a strong resume will act as a valuable point of reference during the interviewing process.

Truth in advertising

In addition to providing a factual representation of your background, your resume serves as an advertisement of your availability.

Although there's no federal regulatory agency like the FDA or FCC to act as a watchdog, I consider it to be ethical common sense to honestly and clearly document your credentials. In other words, don't make exaggerated claims about your past.

The best way to prepare a dynamite resume is not to *change* the facts—just make them more *presentable*. This can be accomplished in two ways:

1. By strengthening the *content* of your resume.

2. By enhancing the *appearance* of your resume.

Remember, your resume is written for the employer, not for you. Its main purpose, once in the hands of the reader, is to answer the following questions: How do you present yourself to others? What have you done in the past? And what are you likely to accomplish in the future?

10 keys to a dynamite resume

To help you construct a better, more powerful resume, here are 10 overall considerations in regard to your resume's content and presentation:

1. **Position title and job description.** Provide your title, plus a detailed explanation of your daily activities and measurable results. Since job titles are often misleading or their function may vary from one company to another, your resume should tell the reader *exactly* what you've done. (Titles such as account manager, business analyst, and internal consultant are especially vague.)

2. **Clarity of dates and places.** Document your work history accurately. Don't leave the reader guessing where you were employed, or for how long. If you've had overlapping jobs, find a way to pull them apart on paper, or eliminate mentioning one, to avoid confusion.

3. **Detail.** Specify some of the more technical, or involved aspects of your past work or education. Have you performed tasks of any complexity or significance? If so, don't be shy; give a one- or two-sentence description.

4. **Proportion.** Give appropriate attention to jobs or educational credentials according to their length, or importance to the reader. For example, if you wish to be considered for a position at a bank, don't write one paragraph describing your current job as a loan officer, followed by three paragraphs about your high school summer job as a lifeguard.

5. **Relevancy.** Confine your *curriculum vitae* to that which is job-related or clearly demonstrates a pattern of success. For example, nobody really cares that your hobby is spear fishing, or that you weigh 137 pounds, or that you belong to an activist youth group. Concentrate on the subject matter that addresses the needs of the employer.

6. **Explicitness.** Leave nothing to the imagination. Don't assume the resume reader knows, for example, that the University of Indiana you attended is in western Pennsylvania, or that an "M.M." is a Master of Music degree, or that your current employer, U.S. Computer Systems, Inc., supplies the fast-food industry with order-taker headsets.

7. **Length.** Fill up only a page or two. If you write more than two pages, it sends a signal to the reader that you can't organize your thoughts, or you're trying too hard to make a good impression. If your content is strong, you won't need more than two pages.

8. **Spelling, grammar and punctuation.** Create an error-free document that is representative of an educated person. If you're unsure about the correctness of your writing (or if English is your second language), consult a professional writer or copy editor. At the very least, use a spell-check program if you have access to a word processor, and always proofread what you've written.

9. **Readability.** Organize your thoughts in a clear, concise manner. Avoid writing in a style that's either fragmented or long-winded. No resume ever won a Nobel Prize for literature; however, an unreadable resume will virtually assure you of starting at the back of the line.

10. **Overall appearance and presentation.** Select the proper visual format, type style, and stationery. Resume readers have become used to a customary and predictable format. If you deviate too much, or your resume takes too much effort to read, it'll

probably end up in the trash, even if you have a terrific background.

Resume writing can be tricky, especially if you haven't done it before. I suggest you write several drafts, and allow yourself the time to proofread for errors and ruminate over what you've written. Practice, after all, makes perfect. If you have a professional associate whose opinion you trust, by all means, listen to what he or she has to say. A simple critique can save you a great deal of time and money.

I worked with a candidate recently who had the most beautifully written resume I've ever seen. When I asked him about it, he said that he sharpened his skills by writing and rewriting his wife's resume. After he got the hang of it, he worked on his own—and kept revising it on a monthly basis.

Building a stronger case

To get the most mileage out of your resume, you'll want to emphasize certain aspects of your background. By doing so, you'll present your qualifications in the most favorable light, and help give the employer a better understanding of your potential value to his or her organization.

You can build a stronger case for your candidacy, by highlighting the following areas of interest:

- **Professional achievements** of particular interest to your reader. For example, if you're in sales, the first thing a hiring manager will want to know is your sales volume, and how it ranks with your peers. If you've won awards, or reached goals, let the employer know. If you're in management, let the reader know the number of people you supervise, and what their titles are.

- **Educational accomplishments**. List your degree(s) and/or relevant course work, thesis or dissertation, or specialized training. Be sure to mention any special honors, scholarships or awards you may have received, such as dean's list, cum laude, or Phi Beta Kappa.

- **Additional areas of competency.** These might include computer software fluency, dollar amount of monthly raw materials purchased or specialized training.
- **Professional designations** that carry weight in your field. If you're licensed or certified in your chosen profession (CPA, CPM or PE, for example), or belong to a trade organization (such as ASTD or ASQC), by all means let the reader know.
- **Success indicators.** You should definitely include anything in your past that might distinguish you as a leader or achiever. Milestones such as Eagle Scout, college class president, scholarship recipient, or valedictorian will help employers identify you as a potential winner. If you worked full-time to put yourself through school, you should consider that experience a success indicator, and mention it on your resume.
- **Related experience.** Anything that would be relevant to your prospective employer's needs. For example, if your occupation requires overseas travel or communication, list your knowledge of foreign languages. If you worked as a co-op student in college, especially in the industry you're currently in, let the reader know.
- **Military history.** If you served in the armed forces, describe your length of service, branch of service, rank, special training, medals and discharge and/or reserve status. Employers generally react favorably to military service experience.
- **Security clearances.** Some industries place a premium on clearances when it comes to getting hired or being promoted. If you're targeting an industry such as aerospace or defense, give your current and/or highest clearable status, and whether you've been specially checked by an investigative agency.
- **Citizenship.** This should be mentioned if your industry requires it. Dual citizenship should also be mentioned, especially if you think you may be working in a foreign country.

In a competitive market, employers are always on the lookout for traits that distinguish one candidate from another. Not long ago, I worked with an engineering manager who mentioned the fact that he was a three-time APBA national power boat champion on his resume. It came as no surprise that several employers warmed up to his resume immediately, and wanted to interview him.

Resume objectives

Most employers find that a carefully worded statement of purpose will help them quickly evaluate your suitability for a given position. An objective statement can be particularly useful as a quick-screen device when viewed by a manager responsible for staffing several types of positions. ("Let's see; accountants in this pile, programmers in that pile, plant managers in that pile...")

While a stated objective gives you the advantage of targeting your employment goals, it can also work against you. A hiring manager lacking in imagination or who's hard-pressed for time will often overlook a resume with an objective that doesn't conform to the exact specifications of a position opening. That means that if your objective reads "vice president position with a progressive, growth-oriented company," you may limit your options and not be considered for the job of regional manager for a struggling company in a mature market—a job you may enjoy and be well suited to.

If you're pretty sure of the exact position you want in the field or industry you're interested in, then state it in your objective. Otherwise, broaden your objective or leave it off the resume.

Getting the dates right

Your employment dates are an important part of your resume. Hiring managers look at dates as a way to evaluate your past performance, and predict your future longevity with their organization.

There are three basic rules governing the way you should document your employment dates:

1. If the average tenure with each of your last three employers has been at least two years, you may simply use *years* to describe your length of stay. For example:

1981 - Present	Ford Motor Company
1974 - 1981	General Motors Corp.
1969 - 1974	American Motors Corp.

2. If the average tenure with each of your last three employers has been less than two years, you should use *months and years*. For example:

5/89 - Present	Tonka Toy Company
1/88 - 4/89	Mattel Toy Company
8/85 - 12/87	Kenner Toy Company

You should also list months and years if you're in your first or second job out of school, or your career has spanned less than three years.

3. Be consistent! Decide which category you're in, and list your dates accordingly. It's best not to mix years with months and years.

If your career has spanned many years, you can summarize your experience prior to a specific date. This can be done in the following manner:

Prior to 1970	Broad-based experience in high-volume manufacturing supervision, specializing in the automotive aftermarket industry.

Here's a tip: If you've changed jobs often (say, twice in the last three years) as a result of layoffs or restructuring, then add a "reason for leaving" heading after each job entry. Although there's a wariness among employers in regard to *job-hopping*, hiring managers will usually empathize with a candidate who's been the victim of a reduction in force. A simply stated "Reason for leaving: manufacturing relocated to Taiwan" will explain the circumstances for your abbreviated tenure with a past employer.

If you made a major career change long ago, don't worry. It's not necessary to document every job you ever had in your former career, since the experience probably won't be relevant to your future employer. Just make sure the dates add up.

Resume arithmetic

I interviewed a candidate recently whose resume showed he earned his undergraduate degree in 1960. So far, so good. But his work history began in 1980. Now, pretend for a moment that you were a hiring manager. Wouldn't this candidate's resume look a little strange to you, since there were 20 years on the resume that were unaccounted for?

Here's another example of the need for resume arithmetic. A few years ago, an aerospace engineer called me to say that after a hiatus of three years, she was ready to get back into the work force. When I asked her to account for the missing years on her resume, she became very defensive, and told me it was none of my business.

She was wrong. It *is* my business. Unfortunately for her, I couldn't help her look for a position, and I seriously doubt any employer would hire her without her first revealing her secret.

Who knows? Maybe she took time off to get a family started. Or maybe she spent three years in federal prison for tax evasion. The point is, most employers will interpret vagueness as a sign that you have something to hide. Given the choice, I'd rather put my cards on the table and take my chances, rather than appear less than candid.

Summary or chronological?

Your resume can be arranged in one of two basic formats: summary or chronological.

1. The *summary* (or *functional*) resume distills your total work experience into major areas of expertise,

and focuses the reader's attention on your accumulated skills.

2. The *chronological* resume presents your skills and accomplishments within the framework of your past employers. (Actually, it should be called a *reverse* chronological resume, since your last job should always appear first.)

Although the information you furnish the reader may essentially be the same, there's a big difference in the way the two resumes are constructed, and the type of impact each will have.

My experience has shown that the chronological resume brings the best results, since it's the most explicit description of the quality and application of your skills within a specific time frame.

The summary resume, on the other hand, works well if you've changed jobs or careers often, and wish to downplay your work history and highlight your level of expertise.

If a prospective hiring manager is specifically interested in a steady, progressively advancing employment history (as most are), then the summary resume will very likely work against you, since the format will seem confusing, and might arouse suspicions as to your potential for longevity.

However, if the employer's main concern is your technical or problem-solving ability, the summary resume will serve your needs just fine.

Either way, you should always follow the guidelines mentioned earlier regarding content and appearance.

Appearance: Always please the reader

In almost all cases, it's best to present as conservative an image as possible, since company hiring managers tend to be creatures of habit. To adhere to the prevailing protocol, select a conventional paper color (white or off-white), weight (24 lb. is standard), texture (a linen or 25-percent cotton bond), and size (8.5 by 11 inches). Be sure to avoid any typeface that would appear flashy or unprofessional, such as a cursive or unusual *sans serif* font.

I've seen resumes that won high marks for creativity, but scored zero when it came to acceptability. Employers expect job candidates to furnish them with a business document, not something that looks like a glitzy brochure or direct-mail piece. Kooky resumes almost always end up in the trash.

Always use plain, unmarked paper, *not your company's stationery*. The only acceptable use of personal or professional letterhead is for follow-up correspondence, such as thank-you letters or letters of acceptance.

A title sheet (a single page with the introduction: "Resume of Gary Burbank...") is redundant, and a waste of paper. It creates a poor impression, and will get ripped off and thrown away. However, you should always be sure to provide your full name, address and home telephone number on the first page, and at least your name on the second page (as in, "Resume of Gary Burbank, Page Two").

A cover letter is unnecessary, unless the employer specifically asks for one in a classified ad, or you need to clarify the intent of your resume submission (such as, "I am writing in response to your ad for the position of accounting manager..."). For all practical purposes, though, your resume's "Objective" will adequately take the place of a cover letter. A cover letter shouldn't be written to strengthen your resume; if your resume is weak, simply rewrite it—a cover letter won't save it.

Here's why you should avoid the temptation to write a cover letter: A poorly written cover letter will hurt your chances of getting hired. For example, I know an advertising executive who routinely disqualifies any candidate whose cover letter contains a typo or misspelling. The point is, why take the risk if you don't have to?

A brief supplement, or *addendum* is acceptable only if the nature of your work is so highly technical or germane to the employer's needs that further explanation of your background is required. Even so, be careful to exercise restraint—a strong resume is all you should need to get your message across.

If you're concerned about confidentiality, you may substitute your company's name with a generic equivalent, such as "Major Dog Food Manufacturer," or "Fortune 500 Financial Institution." However, you should never delete your own name or give an alias.

When mailing a resume, I've found that it's classy not to fold it, but rather to send it flat in a manila envelope. If you have access to a laser printer or nice typewriter, either of these will give you a better result than a dot-matrix printer, which produces copy that is harder to read and becomes fuzzy if the resume is ever photocopied or faxed.

The exception to the conservative approach to resume design might be in the arts, or the communications or advertising professions, where an unusually creative or exotic presentation of your candidacy will rivet the hiring manager's attention.

The key to resume creativity is whether your message will appear in a format the reader can relate to. If you aren't sure of what's appropriate, consult with someone who knows your industry; or simply eliminate the risk and play it straight.

Resume roulette

Earlier, we touched on the subject of ethical common sense. I believe it's foolish and ill-advised to falsify information on your resume, for two reasons. First, you'll be spending the rest of your career perpetuating a lie and worrying about covering your tracks; and secondly, you'll probably be caught sooner or later. Depending on how and when you're found out, the consequences can range from dismissal to litigation, assuming you even make it past the reference checks following your interview.

I know a successful attorney in Los Angeles whose annual salary is predicated on her graduation date from law school. Somehow, her firm got the impression (which she did nothing to correct) that she received her J.D. in 1985, not 1986, her actual date of graduation, and was compensating her accordingly.

Ethics aside, I was amazed at how much time and energy the attorney consumed by worrying about her employer finding out her actual date of graduation. By perpetuating her fraud *ad infinitum*, she managed to tangle her own web to the point where it became nearly impossible for her to confess. My guess is that her guilt will eventually get the better of her, and she'll straighten things out—hopefully before her career suffers irreparable damage.

Here's another aspect of resume pollution to consider: By fraudulently representing yourself, you'll be unfairly denying someone else the chance to compete for a position he or she truly deserves. Spoiling the employment environment is just like spoiling the natural environment—everyone loses in the end.

Before you play resume roulette, think about the long-term consequences of your actions.

How to deal with gray areas

Let's assume you have ethical intentions. Does that mean that you must include every conceivable employment event in your resume? Of course not. There might be some details of your past experience or current circumstances that could work against you if they aren't handled properly.

Remember, it isn't really necessary for an employer to know everything about you, only that which is necessary to make an informed decision regarding your suitability for a particular position.

There are eight gray areas that commonly arise when constructing a resume. Here are some ways to handle them in a professional, ethical manner:

1. **The false start.** Unfortunately, some jobs end after a very brief period, for a variety of reasons. If you were employed for less than about six weeks, I recommend you not mention the short-term job on your resume.

2. **The stopgap job.** Let's suppose you flipped burgers at the local McDonald's to tide you over during a month of unemployment. Do yourself a favor, and leave that experience off your resume.

3. **Extended periods of unemployment.** Chronological gaps of a year or more are almost always noticed—in fact, they tend to draw the attention of most hiring managers. See if you can fill in the dates with any part-time employment or other activities

45

during these periods, as in *IBM Software Consulting* or *Completion of Degree Requirements.*

4. **A "little shy" of graduation.** Never falsify your degree! If you left college without graduating and you hope to finish some day, you may write, "BA Biology Pending Project Completion," or "MBA in progress," or "One hundred twenty-eight credits toward BS Physics."

5. **One more semester to go.** If you're currently enrolled in a degree program, and have a precise graduation date, you may predate or anticipate your degree status, as in, "BSME Candidate; expected graduation: June, 1992," or "BSME, Ohio State University, June, 1992."

6. **Citizenship.** If it doesn't matter to your industry or employer whether you're a U.S. citizen, don't mention it. However, if your name is unusual or sounds foreign, you may want to make note of your U.S. citizenship to avoid confusion.

7. **The green card issue.** Need a sponsor in order to work in this country? Don't draw attention to the fact on your resume until you're called in to interview. Then be completely up front.

8. **Your last date of employment (if unemployed).** To get a little extra mileage, ask your last employer to grant you an extension on your official termination date as a courtesy, even if you're no longer on the payroll. Often, the company will be glad to do this as part of its outplacement service, and you can use the date they give you on your resume.

Your resume is like a TV commercial. While you certainly don't want to mislead the buyer or make exaggerated claims, there's nothing wrong with putting your features in their best light.

Employers expect this, since they know that a resume may be your only chance to get your foot in the door, and appreciate the effort it takes to put together a confident and thoughtfully constructed resume.

Standard categories

Let me suggest some standard categories you can use to organize the material in your resume:

SPECIALIZED TRAINING	PERSONAL
HARDWARE/SOFTWARE	EDUCATION
AWARDS AND HONORS	EXPERIENCE
PROFESSIONAL EXPERIENCE	REFERENCES
WORK HISTORY	ACTIVITIES
PROFESSIONAL AFFILIATIONS	PUBLICATIONS
ADDITIONAL SKILLS	EMPLOYMENT
GRANTS & PROPOSALS	THESIS TOPIC
MILITARY SERVICE	PATENTS
RELATED EXPERIENCE	CERTIFICATIONS
SUMMARY OF QUALIFICATIONS	ACHIEVEMENTS

By compartmentalizing your past experience, you'll help the reader find what he or she is looking for, and draw attention to a particular set of skills or areas of strength.

Beware of artificial fillers and additives

So far, we've talked about ways to enhance or adjust the content of your resume. Now let's look at what should be left out, or at least minimized.

1. **Salary history or salary requirements.** I've never heard one good reason to mention your past, current or expected salary. If you see a classified ad that says, "Only resumes with salary history will be considered," don't believe it. If your resume is strong enough, you'll be contacted. Once contacted, be forthright.

2. **References.** If you have high-impact or well-known professional references, fine. Otherwise, "References: Available Upon Request" will do just fine. Avoid personal references like your minister or your attorney,

unless they happen to be Billy Graham or Sandra Day O'Connor.

3. **Superfluous materials.** When submitting a resume, avoid enclosing such items as your thesis, photos, diplomas, transcripts, product samples, newspaper articles, blueprints, designs or letters of recommendation. These are *props* you can use during your interview, but not before. The only thing other than your resume that's acceptable is your business card.

4. **Personal information.** Leave out anything other than the absolute essentials such as, "Willing to relocate, excellent health." By listing your Masonic affiliation, right-to-life activism or co-dependency support group involvement, you could give the employer a reason to suspect that your outside activities may interfere with your work.

Just the other day, I received a resume from a candidate who felt the need to put his bowling average on the resume. I guess he thought that kind of information might improve his chances of being interviewed. Would I show his resume to an employer? No way.

I can't tell you the number of times I've had to ask candidates to perform major surgery on their resumes. To me, it seems pointless to let candidates run the risk of letting their resumes work against them.

For example, I've seen several resumes in which the candidates misspelled their own names—or listed their birth dates as "1858," or "1991." Wouldn't it be *neat* to work for a 135-year-old boss or train a 2-year-old employee?

The sweet smell of success

Resumes give off a certain *scent* to employers. If for any reason they smell something on a resume that turns them off, the candidate may never get a second chance.

My first experience with a "bloodhound" employer came after only a few weeks in the search business. Working on an assignment for a cloak-and-dagger style aerospace company (in which all employees had to be squeaky clean and top-secret clearable), I mailed in the resume of a superb candidate I'd interviewed in my office. Later, I called Richard, the employer, to get his feedback.

"So, what do you think?" I asked. "Isn't this candidate great?"

"Well, there's no question he can do the job," Richard answered. "But I'm afraid I'm going to pass."

"Pass? You mean you don't even want to interview him?" I asked.

"That's right," replied Richard. "I don't like the affiliations he mentioned on his resume."

"What do you mean? What's wrong with the engineering honor society at UCLA?"

"That's not what I'm referring to," said Richard. "I just don't have a place in my department for someone who belongs to the Sierra Club."

I was stung! I tried for two weeks to convince Richard to reconsider, but in the end, nothing I said helped him overcome his apprehensions (which I don't share, by the way).

The more I thought about it, the more I felt that Richard would've hired the candidate had he not seen the "Personal" portion of the resume, and had never known the candidate belonged to an environmental group. But unfortunately, mentioning it on his resume sounded the candidate's death knell with the company.

The degree of truth

Like many employers, headhunters also have a sixth sense when it comes to resume fraud. As I mentioned earlier, if I spot an educational credential with no date next to it, I automatically assume the candidate's covering something up or falsifying his degree. I'm usually a pretty trusting person, but unfortunately, resume fraud has become all too common.

I've found that verifying a candidate's degree early in the recruiting process can save me a lot of time and embarrassment later. (Headhunters have been sued by employers if the candidates they present are found to have misrepresented their backgrounds. That's why I carry $1 million worth of errors and omissions insurance. I'm hoping the background checks I perform will keep me from ever having to use it.)

The first time I stumbled on a case of resume fraud, I was too naive to realize what was happening. After all, I had no reason to suspect Ted was lying when he told me he had a master's degree in mechanical engineering. And when his *alma mater* said they'd never heard of him, I just assumed they'd fouled up their record keeping. Little did I imagine the wild goose chase that lay ahead.

"Ted, this is Bill calling. I contacted Cal State Long Beach, and they can't find your paperwork anywhere," I reported.

"I can't imagine why not," Ted answered. "Did you call the physics department?"

"Well, no; why should I? Your degree is in mechanical engineering."

"No, no, no. My degree is in physics."

"But you said on your resume it was in mechanical engineering."

"Oh." Ted paused. "Well, they merged the departments. Mechanical engineering's now a part of the physics department."

"Okay, Ted. I'll talk to the physics department."

But of course, they hadn't heard of him either.

"Gosh, I don't know what the problem is," Ted replied when I called him back. "Maybe they have my last name misspelled."

So I tried again, this time using five or six alternate spellings. No luck.

"Well, let's try giving them my social security number," Ted suggested. "That should do it."

But it didn't. By now I was getting a tad suspicious.

"Relax, Bill. The reason you haven't been able to track down my degree is because I got it from the classes I attended at night school. They're kept in a different file."

Oh, sure, that explains it, I thought. So I called the continuing education department. Nothing.

"Ted, I'm a little concerned." I could no longer conceal my irritation. "I must have talked to a dozen different people at Cal State Long Beach, and not a soul has ever heard your name. What's more, my client company's getting nervous. They can't extend you an offer until we can verify your degree."

"Wait a minute," Ted shot back. "Did you say *Cal State* Long Beach? Boy, I'm sorry, there must be a typo on my resume. I got my degree from Long Beach *State*."

I was beginning to smell a rat. But I wanted to give Ted the benefit of the doubt, so I got on the horn to Long Beach State, and we went through the whole thing again—with exactly the same result.

"My friend, I'm going to need some straight answers," I confronted Ted. "If you can't verify your degree, I'm afraid any deal with my client is off."

"Gee, Bill, I was meaning to tell you all along." Ted lowered his voice to a whisper. "I don't actually have a degree. I have the *equivalent* of a degree."

"Oh, that's just great!" I shouted. Boy, was I mad! "Do you mind telling me exactly how many credits you *have* from Long Beach State, or Cal State, or wherever you said you went to school?"

"Credits? Well, uh, the truth is," stuttered Ted, "I don't have any real credits. When I moved to Los Angeles a few years ago, I stopped by a local university, and someone at the front desk told me I had the same work experience as if I had a master's..."

I could have wrung his neck! Not only did he cost me a placement and spoil my reputation with a client, he made a fool of me as well. From then on, I vowed to check references *before* I invested my time helping a candidate get a job.

Play it safe—verify your own degree

Of course, I had another, more personal reason to feel angry—I'd just begun paying back the $20,000 I borrowed to pay for my *own* master's degree. I was outraged that someone could boast a degree they never lifted a finger to get, after I'd made such a sizable investment of time and money.

While I can't claim that every school has a perfect filing system, I've never failed to verify a legitimate degree. After this nasty little incident, I called USC just to make certain my own degree checked out. Sure enough, their records were completely accurate, and my degree is a matter of public record.

If you feel you might have a problem due to an incomplete class, or from failing to pay a campus parking ticket or library fine, my suggestion would be to call the records department or registrar at your *alma mater* and give them your name, social security number, the year you graduated, and your major. They'll be happy to confirm your degree status; and in return, you'll get the peace of mind you deserve.

A resume is such an important part of today's job changing vernacular, it's worth the extra time and effort to get it done right. Given the choice, why not smell like a rose?

> *The keys to a dynamite resume are complete, accurate content and appropriate, professional appearance.*

4 The Resume Test: Good, Better, Best

To demonstrate the power of a dynamite resume (and the effect it'll have on your job search), let's take a moment to examine some actual resumes from my files.

The first three resumes in this chapter were sent to me by recruited candidates who wanted to be considered for a purchasing manager position with one of my client companies. All three candidates were outstanding, and had comparable backgrounds that were well suited to my client's needs. Any one of them could have done the job the employer required, and I felt confident they would all be warmly received.

After an initial telephone presentation, my client, Walter, agreed to come into my office on a Wednesday afternoon to individually interview these three candidates. He requested that I fax their resumes to him for advance consideration.

On Tuesday, the day before the interviews, I called my client. I was interested to know if he had had a chance to study the resumes, and if he had any questions.

Yes, he did. Would I please cancel the interview with candidate number one?

I was puzzled. "Sure, Walter, I'll cancel it," I said. "But his ability is certainly on a par with the other two candidates. Can you tell me what leaves you cold?"

"I can't put my finger on it," he said. "I just don't like his resume. Besides, he doesn't have enough experience."

"Well, how did you like the other candidates?" I asked.

"Candidate number two is better, I suppose. But I like candidate number three the best. He's got the qualifications I'm looking for."

"So, if you were to rank candidates one, two, and three in order, you'd say they were good, better, best."

"Right," said Walter. "Candidate number three is my top choice."

What's behind door number three?

It didn't surprise me that the employer liked candidate number three the best—he had a dynamite resume. Not only was it *filled* with detailed information, the resume was clear, well-organized, and constructed in a way that was pleasing to the eye. It left the reader with no unanswered questions regarding the candidate's education, experience, employment history or job description. It even told the reader what products the candidate's past companies manufactured (extremely important when applying for a purchasing manager position).

In contrast, the resume of candidate number one was listless, confusing and lacking in detail. It failed to command the reader's attention and rambled on in a narrative style. Absent was any mention of professional achievements, such as reductions in cost or inventory; and worst of all, it was written in true (not reverse) chronological order, with the candidate's first job mentioned *first*, not last.

Had candidate number one merely taken the time to thoroughly reveal the full range of his experience and accomplishments (as he did with me when I interviewed him by phone), it would've been crystal-clear to the employer that he was well-suited to compete for the open position. But unfortunately he failed to "sell" himself on the resume by listing his achievements, and this mistake cost him a job interview (and possibly a new job). A real tragedy, in my opinion.

The resume of candidate number two was better—it made the cut. But it lacked the visual appeal and overall organization of resume number one. Resume number two also left a couple of key questions unanswered: What type of products did the candidate's company buy parts to make? And when did the candidate graduate from college?

RAYMOND A. ("BUD") HUNT
224 ELMWOOD PLACE
MARYSVILLE, OHIO 43040
(513) 246-2397

OBJECTIVE: Seeking a Senior Buyer position with a manufacturing company that would utilize my experience and offer an opportunity for advancement.

EDUCATION: B. S. in Business Administration from Eastern Illinois University in Charleston, Il. Majored in Marketing.

EXPERIENCE: DECEMBER 1983 - Began as MRO Buyer for The Hyster Company, an industrial truck manufacturer located in Danville, Il.

JANUARY 1985 - Promoted to Buyer of replacement parts such as springs, seats, fasteners, etc.

DECEMBER 1985 - Promoted to Buyer for new aftermarket program entitled "UNISOURCE". I was one of two buyers assigned to this program which supplied parts to competitive brands of lift trucks. I sourced, and administrated the procurement of, parts ranging from fasteners to bearings to carburetors.

JULY 1986 - PRESENT - Accepted position of Buyer for Koolaire Industries, a refrigeration and air conditioning controls manufacturer located in Lawrence, Kansas. Initially purchased production parts such as electronic coils, metal stampings, and rubber parts, and later assumed responsibility for plastic parts, braze preforms, and springs, among others.
Promoted to <u>Senior Buyer</u> in January, 1991.

ACTIVITIES: Member of National Association of Purchasing Management. I enjoy golf, softball, tennis, and all sports, as well as fishing and camping.

ALEX C. CIRIN

3944 Meadowland Drive
Mason, Ohio 45040
(513) 532-3144

WORK EXPERIENCE AND ACCOMPLISHMENTS

Purchasing Supervisor - Caledon, Inc. (March 1986 to Present)

* **Quoted** unique and special products for nationwide bidding.

* Recommended materials and methods to Engineering to be incorporated into the design to reduce overall product cost.

* **Managed** up to ten buyers, planners and clerks while establishing department **performance goals** and **procedures.**

* Created a **Vendor Policy Manual** outlining quality and delivery performance standards. Consistently improved vendor delivery performance.

* Coordinated planning and purchasing efforts and **improved schedule performance** for cab manufacturing. This represented 30% of Caledon shipments.

* Established **pricing procedures** and manuals to price elevator cabs, entrances and fixtures for Caledon nationwide.

* Created a **Department Manual** including job descriptions and department resonsibilities. Established Purchasing and Receiving procedures for better coordination between plant, jobsite and vendor.

* Initiated training methods and **trained** all levels of department personnel in buying, expediting, computer use, etc.

Senior Buyer - Glengyle Products, Inc. (December 1985 to March 1986)

* Supervised a Junior Buyer, Expediter and Secretary.

* Purchased over $15 million of products per year **saving nearly 20%** on all purchases.

* Implemented the **"Maxcim" computer system** for Purchasing. Trained personnel and created expediting and performance reports to reduce time and manpower.

* Experienced in purchasing nearly all components used by Glengyle Products. Developed new vendors, negotiated blanket contracts, and established strict expediting procedures to improve delivery performance.

<u>Buyer</u> - Glengyle Products, Inc. (February to December 1985)

* Negotiated major contracts for cabs and entrances. Responsible
  for buying many different items.

<u>Buyer</u> - Rotex Inc. (April 1981 to February 1985)

* Organized the Company **United Appeal Drive.** Supervised the Stockroom.
  Investigated Cost Saving Projects. Created procedures for **Inventory
  Control** to interphase with the IBM Computer.

* Acted as Purchasing liaison for the implementation of the **IBM
  System 36.**

* Saved the company thousands of dollars purchasing wood, rubber,
  fasteners, weldments, printing, office products and many other
  items.

* Managed complete purchasing and Inventory Control activity for
  all rubber products.

<u>Junior</u> <u>Buyer</u> - Rotex Inc. (October 1979 to April 1981)

* Saved 10 to 50% by negotiating service, MRO and fasteners contracts.

<u>Inspector</u> - McGill & Smith Engineers (Summers 1977 to 1979)

* Liaison between contractor, County Government and public, protecting
  the interests of all three while seeing that work progressed smoothly
  and safely.

EDUCATION

* M.B.A., Xavier University, International Management, 3.9 GPA.

* Industrial Purchasing and Business Law, University of Cincinnati.

* Seminar Courses: Purchasing, Negotiations, Assertiveness Training,
  MRP II, Kaizen, and Management Training.

* B.A., Hanover College, Major: History, Minor: Economics, 3.94
  GPA, Magna Cum Laude. Helped finance college education with
  summer and on campus jobs.

Chris L. Dahlgren
4568 Woodforest Avenue
Columbus, Indiana 47203
(812) 873-0269

OCCUPATIONAL OBJECTIVE

To obtain a challenging, highly visible Materials/Purchasing
management position within a progressive, quality conscientious
organization.

WORK EXPERIENCE

<u>MULLANE CORPORATION</u> BLOOMINGTON, IN
    Manufacturers of diesel thermostats and temperature control
    products.

Purchasing Manager   1990-Present

* Totally responsible for purchasing, material planning,
  production scheduling, and inventory control; utilizing an
  IBM BPCS AS/400 integrated computer business system.
* Decreased direct material inventory from $2,200,000 to
  $1,400,000 during a 6% growth in sales.
* Reduced direct material rejections by 19%.
* Introduced cost reduction improvements resulting in annual
  savings of $370,000.
* Designed and initiated supplier delivery programs improving
  performance by 49%.
* Developed and implemented a standard cost system.
* Reduced deliquencies by 71% resulting in a "Just-in-time"
  environment.
* Implemented new monitoring systems and control reports into
  computer system.

<u>QUINN & ASSOCIATES, INC.</u> Connersville, IN
    Manufacturers' representative

President/Owner   1989-1990

* Engaged in sales activities representing eight manufacturing
  principals.
* Promoted quality oriented, competitive sources of supply to
  a customer base located throughout the state of Indiana.

<u>WHITE CONSOLIDATED INDUSTRIES, DISHWASHER DIV.</u> Connersville, IN
    Manufacturers of consumer major appliances.

Senior Buyer   1984-1989

* Managed direct procurement activities for raw material and
  custom components in excess of $15,000,000 annually.

* Formulated economically advantaged purchasing contracts and long term business agreements.
* Organized cost reduction development programs resulting in $2,700,000 annual savings.
* Consolidated sources and business opportunities to reduce active supplier base 23%.
* Forecasted and budgeted annual direct material expenditures, capital tooling investments and commodity market activities.
* Accurately predicted relative market trends and positioned requirement procurement activities to either minimize inventory carrying cost or buy futures and inventory consignment policies upon value analysis of economic indicators.
* Evaluated material price variance performance and established action plans to control product cost.
* Surveyed suppliers' performance capabilities in the areas of quality, delivery, R&D support, and cost control programs.
* Performed detailed "Make vs. Buy" value analysis.
* Contributed extensively in the development of a Systematic Deployment (SPD) program.

Material Planner   1975-1984

* Tailored the installation of "MAPICS" inventory management and requirements planning (MRP II) systems by interpreting manufacturing and administrative concerns.
* Initiated inventory management reduction programs that successfully reduced direct material inventory cost from $12,000,000 to $2,500,000.
* Scheduled and expedited material deliveries to support a "Just-in-Time", high volume manufacturing environment.
* Evaluated in-bound traffic lanes to consolidate carriers and successfully negotiated contracts resulting in $1,600,000 annual freight savings.

FORD MOTOR CREDIT CO. Indianapolis, IN
        Automotive Financing

        Account Representative   1972-1975

EDUCATION

Bachelor of Science   Marketing   1972
        Indiana State University
        Terre Haute, Indiana

PERSONAL FACTORS

Birth Date: September 21, 1949   Weight: 170 lbs.
Marital Status: Married   Height: 6'1"
Health: Excellent   Avocations: Golf, Boating

References and additional information furnished upon request.

And so, going into Wednesday's interviewing session, the employer, having been given the choice to interview three excellent candidates of roughly equal ability, had already selected a front runner, put a second on the back burner, and eliminated a third altogether. All based solely on the impressions created by the candidates' resumes!

A resume for all seasons

Let's look at some more dynamite resumes. The following examples will serve to illustrate the common qualities. Even though the candidates' professional experience varies by as much as 30 years, note the similarities in their resumes' construction and style:

- Despite the superficial differences in appearance, they are well-organized, attractive and easy to read.
- Each resume is free of grammatical glitches, typographical mistakes and spelling errors.
- They each draw the reader's attention to the candidate's specific work history, technical skills and major accomplishments.
- They are concise, yet full of specific information prospective employers need to make an evaluation.
- Each one is highly detailed and thorough, and leaves no questions of major importance unanswered.

It may be unfair that the person with a terrific resume has a huge advantage over an equally qualified candidate with an average-looking or poorly done resume. Without bringing a dynamite resume to the plate in the job-changing process, you'll always be batting with two strikes against you.

> *The best resume gives you the best chance for success!*

RICHARD VIZACHERO
2805 Rockford Lane
Cincinnati, OH 45227
(513) 431-5739

OBJECTIVE: Programmer/analyst position in a greater Cincinnati based company with a small to medium size data processing area.

EDUCATION: THE OHIO STATE UNIVERSITY: Columbus, Ohio (1987).
B.S. in Mathematics with special emphasis in business CIS through College of Arts and Sciences.
Business: Managerial and Financial Accounting, micro & macro economics, statistical analysis and computer aided accounting.

EXPERIENCE:

• *CINCINNATI FINANCIAL CORPORATION:*
Programmer   (4/92 to present)

Responsibilities include leading a DB2 conversion project to enhance speed of current system and utilizing all facets of on line and batch queries for reporting and updating purposes. Work on IBM 3090 under MVS using Roscoe with panvelet as the editor.

Languages: Cobol, DB2 and Quickjob. Completed training on MVS and Roscoe. Also utilize Easyflow, a documentation package.

• *HIGHLIGHTS FOR CHILDREN:*
Business Systems Analyst II   (12/90 to 4/92)

Developed new standards and upgraded antiquated systems to meet the newly defined standards. Routinely analyzed and implemented user requests while maintaining current billing and accounting systems.

Conducted projects which included defining user requests, translating them into actual processing requirements and making necessary modifications to accommodate customer needs, including adjusting appropriate documentation.

Languages: Cobol, Easy-trieve Plus, JCL, and Assembler Maintenance. Completed special training program for converting from DOS to MVS.

• *CREDIT BUREAU OF COLUMBUS:*
Programmer/Analyst-Team Leader   (1/88 to 12/90)

Maintained accounting systems which required on-call rotation to ensure successful overnight processing. Co-ordinated projects which included, analysis, design, debugging and documentation of new billing package. Also conducted user training sessions.

Languages: Model 204, Cobol, JCL

PERSONAL: Initiated and coached city league basketball team for 3 years. Also enjoy racquetball, weight lifting, golf and nature.

REFERENCES: Provided upon request

LEE TUCKER

548 Fieldcrest Drive
Cincinnati, Ohio 45255
(513) 860-1697

EDUCATION

BSME, South Dakota State University, Brookings, SD - 1979
EIT - 1979

WORK EXPERIENCE

SUMMARY

Skilled and innovative project engineer with 12 years experience working in small privately owned companies through Fortune 500 companies. Experienced in mechanical design, as well as supervising designers and draftspersons. Proven team player, yet independent when necessary. Experienced in working with customers to develop the products they need. Extremely adept at learning software and programming languages.

DIVERSEY - DUBOIS CHEMICALS INC.   **10-90 to Present**
Cincinnati, OH

Project Engineer

Design and develop chemical dispensing equipment for use in industry and institutions (hospitals, restaurants, etc.). Responsible for all phases of projects including: initial conception, design layout, design, briefing sales and marketing, reviewing production requests for modifications. Usually working on several projects simultaneously.

COOK SCREEN TECHNOLOGIES, INC.   **9-87 to 10-90**
Cincinnati, OH

Senior Project Engineer

Reported to the C.E.O. Responsible for: product design engineering, computer programming, process engineering, manufacturing engineering, computer systems, plant engineering, electrical engineering, and sales engineering. Supervised personnel in the above areas. Involved in company decisions in the above areas.

WCI MACHINE TOOLS AND SYSTEMS INC.   **5-84 to 6-87**
Cincinnati, OH

Project Engineer

Involved in designing new lathes. Worked extensively with CAD/CAM system. Developed multiple machine manufacturing cells. Developed machine design software for personal computer and wrote machine programs. Main interface between electrical engineers and mechanical design engineers. Company probe expert. Trained customers in the use of and programming of probes for in process inspection. Involved with manpower studies, budgeting, project analysis, and other administrative duties.

TAFT-PEIRCE MANUFACTURING COMPANY   9-80 to 5-84
Cumberland, RI

Senior Project Engineer

Supervised draftsmen, detailers, technicians, and lab personnel. Designed and developed prototype CNC control for surface grinder. Redesigned Microstoning machine lines for modular design and construction.

Project Engineer

Managed a $1.2 million project. Involved in design, manufacturing, and customer acceptance.

BENDIX - KANSAS CITY DIVISION   6-79 to 9-80
Kansas City, MO

Product Engineer

Worked in several areas of manufacturing: Supervised sub-assembly manufacturing and testing. Helped develop production techniques on an assembly. Researched microfinishes in small diameter holes.

ORGANIZATIONS

Society of Automotive Engineers

Church Council member 1989, 90, 91
Chairman - Worship Committee - 1991

OTHER INTERESTS

Cincinnati Symphony; Cincinnati Opera; most sports; exotic cars

REFERENCES

Available upon request

DON T. AREN
2346 Millbury Avenue
Reynoldsburg, Ohio 43068
(614) 879-6141

SUMMARY

An innovative executive with eighteen (18) years diversified and progressively responsible experience in purchasing and inventory management. Most recent position includes materials management with responsibility for master planning, production & inventory control, purchasing and materials control.

EXPERIENCE

DIAMOND POWER SPECIALTY COMPANY - Lancaster, Ohio　　　　　　　1984 - Present
(Division of Babcock & Wilcox)
$100 Million Manufacturer of Boiler Cleaning Equipment

<u>Materials Manager</u>　　　　　　　　　　　　　　　　　　　　　　1989 - Present
Responsible for all activities relating to the procurement, production scheduling and expediting, material handling and storage, and inventory control.

- Developed computer generated shop floor job status tracking report which reduced 50 hours per week of manual tracking, enhanced communication between Material Planning and shop floor supervision, and tracked inventory shrinkage problem.
- Improved responsiveness to customer delivery requests by reducing average replacement leadtime on purchased items by 40%. Eliminated need to carry $250,000 in safety stock inventory.
- Developed J.I.T. Raw Material Inventory Reduction Program. Opened up several thousand square feet of shop floor space for productive activities while eliminating associated inventory maintenance costs.
- Created computer generated report which reduced average response time to customer ship date inquiries from one day to one hour.
- Developed computer generated reporting system to define and track slow moving inventory which has resulted in the identification of alternative uses for $1.9 million in materials.

<u>Purchasing Manager</u>　　　　　　　　　　　　　　　　　　　　　1984 - 1989
Responsible for all domestic and international purchasing activities including inventory control on purchased volume exceeding $25 million annually.

- Developed supplier "partnership" program through creation of the Vendor Technical Advisory Committee. Documented cost savings to Diamond Power since 1987 inception exceeds $1.2 million. Presented concept to A.P.I.C.S. National Convention in October of 1989. Articles outlining process published in September 1989 A.P.I.C.S. National Convention Publication and March 1990 issue of Electronics Buyers News.
- Implemented Employee Development Program in line with Purchasing Department's employee career plans.
- Improved on-time delivery performance from 45% in 1985 to current level exceeding 95% through creation of computer generated delivery status and corrective action reports.
- Assisted in the formation of an International Sourcing Network including Asia, Mexico and Western Europe. Vendor sourcing included visits to South Korea, Taiwan, Mexico, Canada, England, Scotland, Spain and France.
- Developed "partnership" concept between supplier community and variety of departments within company through creation of Vendor Information Day and Vendor-Of-The-Year award programs.
- Instituted formalized Cost Savings/Cost Avoidance program resulting in total documented staff savings exceeding $575,000 in latest fiscal year.

64

BAKER C.A.C. - Belle Chasse, Louisiana　　　　　　　1981 - 1983
(Division of Baker Hughes, Inc.)
Manufacturer of Off-Shore Oil Platform Safety Devices

Purchasing/Production Control Manager　　　　　　　1982 - 1983
Responsible for all activities relating to procurement, production scheduling, and expediting.

Purchasing Manager　　　　　　　1981 - 1982

- Reduced purchasing and manufacturing order processing time by 70% and converted Purchasing and Production Control Departments from manual to computer system through implementation of IBM System 38 M.A.P.I.C.S. software package.
- Developed quantitative performance measurements for both Purchasing staff and supplier community through creation of computer generated statistical tracking reports.
- Professionalization of Purchasing Department through reorganization of buyers by commodity classification, development of definitive job descriptions, assignment of individual goals, and required participation in A.M.A. sponsored negotiating seminars.

D-A LUBRICANT COMPANY - Indianapolis, Indiana　　　　　　　1977 - 1981
(Division of Premier Industrial Corp.)

Began as Purchasing Manager with subsequent promotion to Manager of Operations & Procurement for this manufacturer of hydraulic motor oil.

BENDIX MICROWAVE DEVICES COMPANY - Franklin, Indiana　　　　　　　1973 - 1977

Buyer for this manufacturer of electronic devices.

MORRIS PLAN - Indianapolis, Indiana　　　　　　　1971 - 1973

Began as Management Trainee with subsequent promotion to Loan Officer for this savings & loan company.

EDUCATION

B.S. in Business Administration
Bowling Green State University
Bowling Green, Ohio

PROFESSIONAL MEMBERSHIPS

American Production & Inventory Control Society (A.P.I.C.S. Certified)

Purchasing Management Association

JAMES A. ANDERSON

8421 West Bonnie Drive
Mequon, Wisconsin 53092
(414) 321-1892

CAREER SUMMARY

Extensive general management experience in the manufacture of hydraulic, pneumatic, and power transmission products. Significant expertise in:

- New product introductions
- Strategic planning
- Turn-around situations
- Business plan development
- Industrial, military, aerospace markets
- Joint venture management
- Reorganization
- Cost control and down-sizing
- Product safety issues
- Manufacturing technology

EMANON PRODUCTS, Milwaukee, WI (Subsidiary of Okidata, $1.4 Billion)   1986 - Present
$200 million manufacturer of mechanical power transmission equipment.

Vice President Engineering: Director of Corporation
Responsible for all technology functions, customer contract reviews, and product safety and liability concerns. $5.0 million dollar budget, 75 employees.

- Modernized Engineering Department, improving revenue ratios per employee from $220,000 to $560,000 in five years.

- Promoted company-wide cost reduction program resulting in $10 million annual savings. Reduced engineering expenses from 4.3% to 2.4% of sales.

- Introduced two new technologies: Metal Matrix Composites and Variable Reluctance Motors.

- Served as General Chairman for Sundstrand's Industrial Group Technical Enhancement Program and chaired Materials and Power Transmission sub-committees.

- Visited numerous foreign companies, exploring potential for joint venture relationships.

Outside Professional Activities

- Chairman of the Industrial Liaison Council, University of Wisconsin - Milwaukee College of Engineering and Applied Science.

- Active in Gear Research Institute and American Gear Manufacturers' Association. Appointed to American Bureau of Shipping, Panel on Gears.

WESTERN GEAR CORPORATION, Everett, WA (Division of Becor Western, $400 million)   1982 - 1986
$40 Million manufacturer of gearing, hydraulic, electronic, and pneumatic systems.

Manager of Engineering
Responsible for all technical functions, including functional/strategic planning and budgeting. Supervised staff of 80 people with annual budget of $3.0 million, serving petroleum, defense, and steel industries.

- Directed design team to 22% increase in productivity.

- Introduced two new products to the market place: Long Stroke Pumper and High Efficiency Drill String Compensator, used in on-shore and off-shore applications.

- Established corporate-wide technical resource sharing agreements, saving $600,000 in expenses during first year implemented.

page two

PETRO MARINE ENGINEERING, INC., Houston, TX   1980 - 1982
Offshore structures and marine engineering consulting firm of approximately 400 engineers worldwide.

Manager of Engineering
Directly supervised staff of 50 multi-disciplined engineers and drafters engaged in design of offshore oil platforms and drilling vessels. Negotiated licensing, technical, and financing agreements with foreign and domestic clients for the design and construction of drilling vessels.

HYDROTECH SYSTEMS, INC., Houston, TX   1973 - 1980
Pipeline products manufacturing/service company; $17 million in sales; acquired by Hughes Tool Company in 1980.

Executive Vice President; Chief Operating Officer
P & L responsibility over all domestic and foreign operations, employing 150 people.

- Organized global engineering and marketing efforts, pioneering mechanical subsea pipeline connections in the petroleum industry.

- Managed 5 year joint venture company in partnership with Norwegian Corporation serving Philips Petroleum.

- Awarded four U.S. Patents on new designs; received Meritorious Engineering Award from Offshore Technology Conference, 1978.

RUCKER CONTROL SYSTEMS, Oakland, CA/Houston, TX   1968 - 1973
Manufacturer of hydraulic and pneumatic systems for offshore oil industry. (Currently NL Petroleum Group)

Product Manager/Design Engineer for Offshore Motion Compensation/Tensioning Systems
Responsible for marketing motion control equipment to offshore drilling industry. Awarded U.S. Patents on four standard products which revolutionized offshore drilling industry and increased sales of equipment from $1.5 million/year to $40 million/year in four years. Hold patents on Drill String Compensator which was profiled in Fortune and Smithsonian magazines.

LAWRENCE RADIATION LABORATORY, Berkeley, CA   until 1968
U.S. Government laboratory run by University of California

EDUCATION

- *University of California*, Berkeley, California
  Bachelor of Science degree - Mechanical Engineering
- *Northwestern University*, Evanston, Illinois
  Mechanical Engineering major
- Pi Tau Sigma, Engineering Honor Society
  University of California - Berkeley
- Tau Beta Pi, Engineering Honor Society
  University of California - Berkeley
- Dean's Honor Roll
  University of California - Berkeley
- Licensed Professional Mechanical Engineer, California, Expert Witness

```
ROBERT BODLEY                          3408 Packer Road, #303A
708-335-5781                           North Chicago, IL  60064
```

Objective: **SALES and/or MARKETING MANAGEMENT.**

Proficiencies: Direct Account Sales   Sales Force Building & Management
                    Strategic Planning   Purchase Contract Negotiation
                    Market Assessment   New Business Development
                    Product Promotion   Forecasting & Budgeting

Experience:

Jul 89 - Feb 91   **ORANGE ELECTRICAL PRODUCTS**, Waukegan, Illinois
Multi-national corporation manufacturing precision switches, electroluminescent flat panel displays, gas plasma displays, keyboards and high volume custom electronic assemblies.

<u>Sales & Marketing Manager</u>, Electronics Division
Reported to General Manager. Responsible for division sales, forecasting, management of sales force, direct handling of target accounts plus determining product and market directions.

* Focused division marketing and sales efforts on the product lines that showed the greatest potential for achieving 100% overall revenue growth by 1993.

* Pushed dot matrix gas plasma display development program ahead to boost product line into $30M low resolution market. Pursued added value electronics with display opportunities.

* Broadened the growth potential for the division's electronic assembly capabilities by targeting the high volume operator interface control panel and custom electronic module markets.

Jan 83 - Jun 89   **DISC INSTRUMENTS**, (Honeywell subsidiary), Costa Mesa, California
Manufacturer of optoelectronic incremental shaft encoders, trackballs and other computer peripheral input devices.

<u>Marketing Director</u>
Reported to General Manager. Promoted from sales management role to position with overall responsibility for strategic marketing, product planning and sales operations.

* Expanded trackball product line to include desktop trackball as alternative to the mouse, and championed development of image manipulator (dial set) for 3-D real-time modeling graphics workstation market niche.

* Increased sales of trackballs and peripheral input devices over 280% in the three years following the introduction of the desktop trackball and the dial set peripheral.

* Negotiated the largest two OEM encoder purchase agreements in company history producing revenue in excess of $6.2M.

* Contracted optical encoder market survey to determine long range trends resulting in program for advanced product design and manufacturing process development to reduce costs by 65%.

Feb 82 - Jan 83   **BEI ELECTRONICS, INC.**, Santa Ana, California
Multi-division manufacturer of optoelectronic incremental and
absolute encoders for industrial and military applications.

<u>Western Regional Sales Manager</u>
Reported to corporate VP of Marketing.   Responsible for
regional sales of all products from each of the three
manufacturing divisions.

* Set up regional sales office, hired support staff and worked
  with the sales manager of each division to reverse downward
  sales trend in western region.

* Directly handled all major accounts in region and exceeded
  1982 sales goal by 12% aided by technical background and
  prior encoder experience.

* Generated in-depth technical product application notes for
  use as sales tools to foster customer confidence in company.

Oct 78 - Feb 82   **DISC INSTRUMENTS, INC.**, Costa Mesa, California
Manufacturer of optoelectronic incremental shaft encoders.

<u>National Sales Manager</u>
Reported to Marketing Director. Responsible for domestic sales
and for hiring, training and managing of the direct sales force.

* Increased sales an average of 24% annually. Brought sales
  up from $4M to $10M in first three years with company.

* Provided technical support to field salespeople and product
  applications assistance to customers.

* Developed sales programs to increase penetration into and
  share of the industrial, medical, instrumentation and
  computer peripheral markets.

* Implemented new product cost estimating system to speed up
  pricing process and provide more competitive quotations.

* Improved field sales incentive program to reward for new
  accounts as well as for quarterly bookings performance.

Prior to Oct 78   **GOULD, DATA TECHNOLOGY, ALLEGHENY STEEL and WESTERN ELECTRIC**
Various sales and engineering positions with the above firms.

Education: Stanford University, AEA Stanford Executive Institute, 1984
Northeastern University, Engineering Management, 1970-72
Worcester Polytechnic Institute, BSEE, 1960
Various Business Management, Sales and Marketing Seminars

Member of IEEE - Knowledgeable PC user - Willing to travel extensively

MICHAEL SHARFE

102 Bethany Avenue
Glen Burnie, Md 21060
(301) 761-4896 (H)
(301) 423-2397 (W)

EDUCATION

MASTER OF SCIENCE, MECHANICAL ENGINEERING. West Virginia Institute of Technology, Montgomery, WV. December 1987. Concentration in Thermal Science and Fluid Mechanics. Thesis topic: *"Transient Enthalpy Modeling of a Phase Change Heat Storage System."* Simulation of system's transient behavior via Finite Difference Techniques.

BACHELOR OF SCIENCE, MECHANICAL ENGINEERING. West Virginia Institute of Technology, Montgomery, WV. May 1985

SPECIALIZED TRAINING

FINITE ELEMENT BASED SOFTWARE FOR COMPUTATIONAL FLUID DYNAMICS AND HEAT TRANSFER (FIDAP).

TRAINED AND CERTIFIED IN "QUALITY ENGINEERING BY DESIGN-THE TAGUCHI APPROACH". Design of Experiments Techniques. Rochester Institute of Technology, 1989

EXPERIENCE

R&D Engineer. Bowles Fluidics Corporation Columbia, Md. (4/89 - Present).
* Research and development of fluidic devices actuated via air and fluid flow for new product development.
* Responsible for resolving technical problems related to product performance, design and execution of controlled experiments, failure analysis.
* Finite element techniques utilized for analyzing the transient behavior of various turbulent flow fields and heat transfer.
* Responsible for facilitating Design of Experiments Techniques (Taguchi Approach) related to product design and injection molding processes.

Senior Engineer. Dynatherm Corporation Cockeysville, MD. (1/88-4/89).
* Research and development in heat pipe technology and various thermal and mechanical systems related to space and terrestrial applications, for NASA and private industry.
* Component development for spacecraft temperature control, thermal modelling and testing of heat transport systems, heat exchanger design, porous media, fluid flow.
* Experience with both low (refrigerants) and high (liquid metals) temperature applications, stress analysis.

Other Related Positions. West Virginia Tech, (8/85-12/87).
* Research Assistant. Research on heat pipe effective thermal conductivity, start up from frozen state.
* Adjunct Instructor of Mathematics. Taught Analytic Geometry, Pre-Calculus, Algebra, Trigonometry.
* Supervisor and lecturer, Heat & Mass Transfer lab. Conducted experiments in conduction, free/forced convection, radiation, and heat exchangers.

ADDITIONAL SKILLS

Proficient in Basic, Fortran, various word processing software, lotus, macro development, Autocad.

ACTIVITIES
* President / Founder of Graduate Student Organization (G.S.O) (85-87).
* Student Representative, Graduate Committee (85-87).
* Associate member of ASME

REFERENCES

Available upon request

Louis A. Lausche
1822 Castle Drive
Statesville, NC 28677
Telephone: 704-922-4521

Objective
An engineering position where skills acquired through education and experience can be utilized to contribute to the organization's success and advancement is based on performance.

Professional Experience

Design/Development Engineer (June 1989 to Present)
Clark-Hurth Components, Statesville, NC
Designs and manufactures power transfer systems for the heavy-duty off-road OEM market (Axles and Transmissions)

- Responsibilities in Axle Engineering include:
- Evaluate applications and analyze selected product performance
- Optimize axle designs for reliability and cost
- Conduct laboratory and field tests to verify design and improvements
- Develop new product designs to meet changing customer requirements
- Apply modern analytical techniques and develop standard procedures
- Furnish technical support to plant and vendor machining and assembly
- Incorporate computer techniques to improve productivity

Mechanical Design Engineer (July 1983 to June 1989)
General Electric Company, Ordnance Systems Division, Pittsfield, MA
Designs and manufactures hydromechanical transmissions for tracked vehicle applications

Responsibilities in Production Engineering included:
- Designed improvements in the 21 in^3 ball piston pump/motor unit
- Reduced cost of transmission components
- Increased reliability of hydraulic and mechanical components
- Conducted laboratory and field tests to verify design improvements
- Participated in Future Product Design Team for hydraulic units
- Analyzed component failures using FEA
- Provided technical support to assembly, machining and vendors

Analytical Skills
Machine Design, Gear Design, Weibull Analysis, Fluid Analysis, Tribology

Computer Skills
Computer Analysis (Macintosh, IBM, HP, DEC); Computer Programming (BASIC, FORTRAN); Finite Element Analysis (PATRAN, ANSYS, ABAQUS)

Education
MSME (May 1986) Rensselaer Polytechnic Institute, Troy, NY
BSME (June 1983) Union College, Schenectady, NY

Seminars

Professional Engineer Exam Review, UNC, Charlotte, NC	Jan. '91
Kepner-Tregoe Problem Analysis, Clark, Statesville, NC	Dec. '90
Fastener Technology, Clemson, Greenville, SC	June '90
Fundamentals of Gear Design, UW, Milwaukee, WI	Dec. '89
Aries Workstation Training, GE, Pittsfield, MA	Jan. '89
Value Engineering Analysis, GE, Pittsfield, MA	Jan. '88
Process Planning and Analysis, GE, Pittsfield, MA	Jan. '87

References Available on Request

5 Your Compensation: Let's Get Real

As a headhunter, the most frequently asked question I get is: "What sort of salary increase can I expect when I change jobs?"

Here's my reply: That depends; we live in a market dictated by supply and demand.

Given the current economic conditions, employers generally calculate a salary increase for an experienced professional based on his or her previous earnings, not on artificial pay grades, or what a particular position is "worth."

Unless you're grossly underpaid, or you're reentering the work force, the standard increase is between 3 percent and 8 percent for salaries under $100,000 per year.

There are exceptions, of course. But unless your past record of professional accomplishments is certifiably extraordinary (or there's an incredibly high demand for your type of skills), don't be disappointed by a standard increase.

Think of your base salary as being in a *range* of either low, mid or high. That is, a salary of $32,000 is in the "low 30s," a salary of $35,000 is in the "mid 30s," and a salary of $38,000 is in the "high 30s." For practical purposes, a round number like $40,000 would be considered to be in the "low 40s."

If you think in these terms, it's usually realistic to receive an increase in which you *bump* a range, say from "high 40s" to "low 50s." (Above $100,000, the range of increase is more often determined by *percentage*.)

How to figure your total package

Base salary, of course, is only one dimension of your overall compensation. To complete your *salary preparations,* consider these additional factors that may affect your total package:

- **Health and dental insurance.** How much is your company-paid insurance worth to you and your family each year? Do you pay a monthly contribution? If so, factor in that amount.

- **Profit sharing.** How much did you receive in the form of distributions over the last year?

- **Pension plan.** Does your company offer a 401(k) plan? If so, how much is it worth to you as a tax shelter, and in terms of direct, company-paid contributions?

- **Retirement.** If you're not already vested, will you forfeit any money by leaving your present employer?

- **Life insurance.** Are you covered by your present company? How much would you have to pay to receive the same coverage?

- **Company-paid disability.** Are you covered? If so, for what amount? What's the premium worth to you on an annual basis?

- **Company car and/or gas credit card.** If these are a part of your package, how much are they worth to you per year?

- **Travel allowance.** Does your company pay you a fixed monthly sum?

- **Tuition reimbursement.** Is your company helping to further your education? If so, what's the dollar amount of its contribution?

- **Cash bonuses.** Are you being rewarded for a job well done? If so, what amount did you receive in the past year?

- **Overtime or hazard pay.** What was it worth to you last year?

- **Day care**. Do you work for a progressive company that provides this valuable service? If so, how much money did you save by taking advantage of it?

On the other hand, what's it costing you to work at your current job? Let's look at some frequently overlooked employee expenses:

- **Commuting by private vehicle**. How much money do you spend to maintain, repair and fuel your car?

- **Toll charges**. Do you travel by turnpike or across a toll bridge to work? What does it cost you?

- **Parking**. How much do you have to pay to park your car?

- **Insurance**. Many auto insurance companies charge you a higher premium if you live in the suburbs and work in the city. (This practice is known as *redlining*.) What's the differential, if any?

- **Public transportation**. Do you commute by bus, rail or rapid transit? How much do you spend?

- **Cost of living**. Do you live in an area with an inflated cost of living? If so, how much more are you paying in housing? In taxes? In services? In utilities? In schooling for your children?

- **Long-distance telephone charges**. Do you make business calls from home or on the road that aren't being reimbursed?

- **Tools of the trade**. Does your job require you to use a computer at home, or a modem, or a fax? What are you paying for the hardware, the software and the supplies?

Before you put yourself on the market, you should have these numbers ready, so you know your precise remuneration. I'm not suggesting you become obsessive about compensation— you just want to know what you're actually earning, so you can make an accurate comparison when contemplating an offer.

Remember that these variables work both ways. For example, you may find that a seemingly "low" offer may actually represent an increase; while accepting an apparent "windfall" salary offer may leave you in worse shape than before!

The art of the deal

Not too long ago, I worked with a candidate who was earning $45,000 a year as a programmer. The candidate was very reasonable in his salary expectations; as long I could find him a new job that gave him the opportunity to develop his skills, he would be willing to accept a *lateral* offer.

Because he was already earning the reasonable and customary industry maximum for his level of experience, I asked him this question when we first discussed his salary needs: As long as I can get you $45,000 in *first-year total compensation,* would that be acceptable to you? His answer was yes.

Two weeks later, one of my clients wanted to make him an offer. They'd interviewed him twice, checked his references, and felt certain he'd be a valuable asset to their company, a large, well-known manufacturer of machine tools.

But because of the prevailing salary structure within the company, they couldn't bring him on board for a penny more than $40,000 a year. Luckily, the employer, Art, was a pretty creative manager.

"Gee, Art," I said. "If only you could up the ante, I'm sure my candidate would accept your job offer."

"I'm really sorry," Art shrugged. "If we go any higher than $40,000, it'll upset the whole department, and I'll have a mass exodus on my hands."

"That could get ugly. But isn't there *something* we can do?"

"Let me give it some thought and I'll call you back. Will you be in your office later today?"

"Sure," I said, wondering what magic formula Art might have up his sleeve.

A couple of hours later, the phone rang. It was Art.

"Bill, didn't you tell me the candidate lived an hour outside the city?" Art asked.

"That's right."

"Well, I'll tell you what. I'll throw in a gas credit card plus routine maintenance on his car. That would be worth about $1,500 a year, right?"

"Sure, because he'd be commuting about 30,000 miles a year."

"And we can pay him overtime, at time and a half. If he works two extra hours a week at $30 an hour, that's an extra $3,000 a year. And we'll make it easy for him—we'll loan him a PC and a modem so he can work overtime from home."

"That sounds great," I said. "But we're still $500 short."

"True, we are." Art paused. "Maybe we can't put this deal together after all."

"Wait a minute, I have an idea. His present company has a 401(k) plan, but it's non-contributory. What does your 401(k) plan provide?"

Art chuckled. "I think we found the answer. Our plan matches his contribution dollar for dollar up to $3,000. All he'd have to do is contribute $10 a week, and he'd earn an extra $520 a year, tax-free. Do you think he'll accept our offer now?"

"We can give it the old college try," I said. "And thanks for finding a way to put this together."

Sure enough, the candidate accepted the offer, and was flattered that my client company thought enough of him to figure out a way he could make the money he needed without making waves within the department.

Getting started: Timing is everything

Although a job change can occur very quickly under the right circumstances, it's best to allow three months or so for the process to develop. Ample time must be allowed in order to prepare a resume, schedule interviews, meet with prospective employers, accept an offer, give two weeks' notice and settle into a new place of work.

Therefore, common sense dictates that you should have all your ducks in a row before you begin your job-changing campaign in earnest. Before you get the ball rolling, check to make sure that poor planning won't inhibit a smooth flow of events.

A Job-Changer's Checklist

Within the next three months, will you have:

Yes	No	
❑	❑	An unpredictable or unusually heavy work schedule?
❑	❑	Any work-related travel?
❑	❑	A vacation or any personal trips planned?
❑	❑	Any prearranged medical treatment or maternity leave?
❑	❑	Any job commitments, such as a project deadline?
❑	❑	Any school commitments, such as exams or graduation?
❑	❑	Any personal or family obligations?
❑	❑	An annual review or other scheduled evaluation?
❑	❑	Any other reason you can't start a new job within two to four weeks of an accepted offer?

If the answer is "yes" to any of the questions on the job-changer's checklist, you have a choice: You can either work around your previous commitments, or postpone your activity until a more suitable time.

Some occupations are *time-sensitive,* or have built-in seasonal considerations. Accounting, hospitality and retail management often adhere to industry-driven schedules, and can become frenzied at certain times of the year. The month of April, for example, might not be the best time to seek another position as a tax accountant. If your search targets a seasonal industry, be sure to give some thought as to whether the timing of your job search is appropriate.

I once worked with a job-seeker who said he'd be available to start with a new company immediately. Later, after he accepted my client's job offer, he announced his intention to delay his start date for six months so that he could do missionary work in New Zealand. The trip had been scheduled for over a year, he explained; he simply "forgot" to tell me about it. Unfortunately for the candidate, my client withdrew his offer.

Travel advisory

Travel commitments aren't always an impediment to your job change. Often, you can put your mobility to good use.

If you know you're going to be in a metropolitan area where you have an interest in relocating (or you'd like to try a "test trip"), set up interviews in advance, letting your contacts know when you'll be arriving.

Employers are far more receptive to this approach than they are to arranging for a special interviewing trip. Besides saving them money, it lets them know of your sincere interest in moving to their city, and puts you on equal status with other local candidates who may also be under consideration.

Relocation: The hidden costs

It goes without saying that any expenses you incur from a physical move will affect your first-year compensation. And if you're fortunate enough to have a new employer pay your relocation, great.

But beware: Unless the new company can adequately compensate you for your relocation expenses, you could be hit pretty hard at tax time.

Here's why. Let's suppose you live in North Carolina and you accept a new job in Texas. After your move, in accordance to your relocation agreement, the Texas company cuts you a check to cover the cost of the physical move. "Hey, this is terrific," you say, as you run to the bank to deposit the check.

But wait! That check is reported to the IRS as miscellaneous income, which means you have to pay taxes on it. So instead of breaking even, you're now paying your personal tax bracket's share for the privilege of moving.

Many companies now have relocation packages that address this issue, and will *gross-up* your earnings to take the bite out of your tax liability. If you ever deal with an employer that doesn't, try to estimate expenses and add the differential to your balance sheet, or ask your new employer if there's anything they can do to soften your newly acquired tax burden.

To a home owner, relocation expenses involve a whole lot more than simply paying the moving company. Try to include your closing costs and points in any relocation package. If you decide to rent your old house, estimate any negative cash flow or additional taxes that may result.

If you're not sure whether your salary compares favorably with others in your industry, check out *The American Almanac of Jobs and Salaries* by John Wright (Avon, 1991). Or, scan the periodical database in your local library for industry-specific salary surveys. These resources should give you a pretty good idea of whether you're being compensated according to industry standards.

Careful consideration of your total compensation and relocation costs will greatly facilitate your job change.

6 Placing Yourself on the Job Market

I have a good friend named Andy York. The other day, Andy called me, and wanted to get together over a cup of coffee for some professional advice. It seems he's been looking for a new job for more than a year, but without success.

"I just can't seem to make any progress," Andy lamented. "I know I have a good background, but no one seems interested."

"How do you mean?"

"Well, I'll give you an example of something that happens again and again. About a month ago, I mailed a resume in response to an ad I saw in the Sunday classifieds. So far, I haven't even gotten a 'thanks, but no thanks' letter in return."

"Are you qualified for the position?"

"The fit may not be perfect, but I know I can do the job. And my paperwork looks good," he said, handing me his resume.

Sure enough, his resume wasn't the problem; it was concise and very professional-looking. "You're probably up against some stiff competition," I said. "Or the company's dragging its feet. In either case, I'd suggest you intensify your approach."

"I think you just lost me."

"It would be easier to explain," I said, "if I could convince you to do a little role-playing with me."

"I'm game."

"All right. Pretend you're the hiring manager at the company you sent your resume to and I'll be you, the candidate."

"I can do that."

"OK. Ready? Begin!"

Manager: Ring, ring, ring. Hello, this is the manager at ABC Company.

Candidate: Mr. Manager, my name is Andy York. You and I have never spoken, but I'm calling in the hope that we'll both benefit from our conversation. Is this a good time to talk?

Manager: Sure, go ahead.

Candidate: I'm currently working as a project leader for a company that's a direct competitor of yours. Partly as a result of my efforts, my department has grown in size, and my company has increased its productivity over the last year by nearly 70 percent.

I don't know if my timing's right, but I'd like to talk to you about the things I've done to help my company become more profitable, and how my skills might have an impact on your organization, should I ever go to work for you.

Please don't misinterpret my call—I'm not necessarily asking you for a job. But I *do* think it would be a good idea to explore any common interests we might share. What are your thoughts?

Manager: Well, Andy, why don't you send your resume to our personnel office, and we'll get in touch?

Candidate: That's exactly the reason I called. My curiosity was piqued when I saw your ad a few weeks back; but evidently the resume I sent fell through the cracks. I'm certain if you and I were to talk, there'd be absolutely no question as to my potential value to your company. Is there a convenient time this week when I can stop by?

Manager: Sure. How about Thursday?

Candidate: Fine. I'll see you about 1 p.m.

"Wait! That sounds like a sales job!" snorted Andy.

"You could call it that, I suppose. But look at what the call accomplished. You spoke directly with a decision-maker and scheduled a job interview with a company you'd like to work for. What's so bad about that?"

"Well, it's so *assertive*. I'd feel uncomfortable calling a total stranger."

"Exactly; that's what makes cold calling so unpopular. But consider the alternative—sitting around like a wallflower while the assertive people dance. Sometimes, it takes more than just licking a stamp to get what you really want."

Walking it through the maze

Have you ever felt like Andy? I have. It's as if you rolled up your resume, corked it in an old Dr. Pepper® bottle, and pitched it in the ocean. And now you're standing on the beach, praying that someday, someone might find it and get in touch.

Personally, I need to feel like I have more control. The script I just role-played with Andy is one that's worked wonders for me over the years, both as a recruiter and as a candidate on the job market. I suggest you use it a week or two after waiting for your Dr. Pepper® bottle to return. By calling the employer directly, you can rescue your candidacy from the employer's complacency—or misinterpretation of your skills.

Occasionally, you'll be thwarted in your effort to directly follow up on a job notice published in the "help wanted" section of the newspaper. Employers will sometimes run a *blind box ad* (in which the only address given is a post office box) when they want to protect the identity of their company. They may do this for several different reasons:

- They don't want to be besieged with telephone calls from candidates.
- They don't want their competitors to know they're in a hiring mode.
- They don't want an *incumbent* (someone they wish to replace) to find out they're conducting a search.

- They want to set a trap for their own employees, to see if any of them answer the ad. (Corporate paranoia is rare, but it does exist.)
- They wish to use the responses of job seekers as market research data to get a feel for such issues as salary, education and availability of the current talent pool.

One way to discover the identity of the blind box employer is to make an educated guess based on any clues you might have picked up from the ad. Call the company you suspect might have run it, and ask for the personnel department. Tell them that you wish to apply for the position they advertised in the Sunday paper. With any luck, they will have forgotten that it was a blind box ad they ran. Then you can proceed to present your background to the appropriate manager.

Depending on others to take action is one way to lose control in your job campaign. Unfortunately, many companies tend to behave like staid, lethargic bureaucracies when faced with the task of hiring people. I've found that with all the twists and turns in the process, the best approach may be to take your resume and "walk it through" the employment maze yourself. That way, it's less likely to get lost in the shuffle.

The power of peripheral vision

The positions listed in classified newspaper ads represent only a fraction of the potential opportunities available to you. In fact, employment experts agree that as many as 85 percent of all job openings aren't even advertised.

To keep your options open, it's a good idea to widen your field of vision when it comes to locating another position. You'll find that job openings abound, if you know where to look. Consider these sources:

- **Electronic job listings** furnish the up-to-date hiring needs of a wide range of companies. Unlike classified ads, they tend to be more highly descriptive of both the job and the hiring company. One such listing service, Adnet Online, advertises about 2,000 current job openings, and serves the 3.5 million subscribers of PC networks like Prodigy, CompuServe, GEnie, America Online and a number of smaller networks.

- **Clipping services** compile classified ads and reprint them on a periodic basis. *The National Business Employment Weekly*, for example, contains employment notices published in *The Wall Street Journal,* and can be found in bookstores, or may be purchased through subscription.

- **Industry journals, bulletins and newsletters** regularly supply their readers with notices of help wanted, and furnish information that's of particular interest to their audiences. Look for publications that serve your industry, such as *Personnel Management* and *Accounting Review.* In addition, the authors of each magazine's editorials and technical articles are often employers, and you can call them directly to ask for help in your search for an opening that matches your background.

- **Trade magazines** also run help-wanted ads, and the display ads placed by companies offering products or services to the magazine subscribers should give you some clues as to who might be hiring. Publications such as *Computer World* and *Material Handling Engineering,* for example, provide an excellent source of leads in those industries.

The first time I saw a copy of *SENSORS* magazine, I was sitting in the reception area of a client's office. I couldn't believe my eyes! Here was an engineering magazine dedicated to my own high-tech niche market, filled with display ads placed by highly specialized companies I'd never heard of. Eventually, I contacted these companies to see if they needed to hire more people to support their new products' research, development, marketing, sales, manufacturing, quality control or distribution. Not surprisingly, some of the companies I contacted became my clients, and hired the people I referred.

Naturally, you can use reverse psychology, and advertise your own availability in these types of publications. Many of them have "positions wanted" sections that are free to subscribing members. Or, you can pay a fee to run a classified ad in your local business newspaper.

Alternative sources of job leads

The hunt for job openings can be an exciting adventure. All you need is a little creativity, and the ability to view every magazine article or display ad as a job lead in disguise. To get some ideas, take a look at the following resources:

- **Local business weeklies** provide the latest gossip on the movers and shakers in your home town, and regularly profile a variety of local companies. Headlines that read, "Bahunkus Corporation Expands Office Space," or "Local Dress Company Adds New Product Line" should provide you with clues to those companies' possible hiring needs.
- **Industry directories** such as *Who's Who in Electrical Engineering* or *The International Pulp and Paper Directory* catalog most of the companies within a narrowly defined industry, plus the names of individuals who can be contacted for information.
- **Buyer's guides** list the suppliers that serve the needs of various industries, and list hundreds of companies who may have job openings. For example, take a look at *The Optical Industry & Systems Purchasing Directory* or *The Modern Plastics Encyclopedia*. Does your industry make use of such a guide, or advertise in one?

Try networking through your personal contacts, such as your family, friends, acquaintances, and people you know from work, especially those who've changed jobs themselves.

Expanding your network

Active participation in group activities is one of the best ways to get noticed and gather useful ideas for your search.

You might start with your local chamber of commerce or Rotary Club; these types of organizations tend to attract managers and other company officials like prospectors to a gold strike.

Simply attend their meetings and stake your claim. These groups often sponsor special "networking" events at which those in attendance are encouraged to mingle and swap business cards.

Some people I know have formed loosely knit networks of industry professionals who meet periodically for the purpose of exchanging business ideas and expanding their number of contacts. If you're so inclined, you can organize your own group. At the very least, keep your eyes open: these types of groups usually post notices of their upcoming meetings in the local newspaper or business magazines.

Specialty, professional or trade organizations also provide a terrific vehicle for networking. I belong to a couple of groups that are fairly typical: The Instrument Society of America and the Society of Weighing and Measurement. Associations like these hold regular dinner meetings, workshops, demonstrations and lectures; and membership in the organization gives you the opportunity to swap job leads with others in your profession.

If you have any doubt about the number or variety of such groups, simply go to your local library and look in the ***Encyclopedia of Associations***. You'll find more than 22,000 entries, which range from the generic (The American Business Women's Association) to the specific (The Association of Industrial Lighting Distributors) to the esoteric (The Society of Biological Psychiatry).

Trade shows, conferences and conventions also provide a conspicuous meeting ground for those in your industry. Usually, there's a bulletin board with job listings near the convention hall entrance; and in the back section of the exhibitor directory, you're likely to find a listing of employment opportunities.

Naturally, recruiters and hiring managers are no strangers to such gatherings; they can be found trolling the conference floor, fishing for industry talent.

Don't forget the job fairs

Job fairs represent the most direct way to meet prospective employers and to get your resume into circulation. By taking part, you'll not only get a chance to talk to hiring managers, you'll also be able to meet other job-changers you can network with later. If you like, the sponsors of each job fair you visit will make sure your resume finds its way into the hands of other interested parties, such as additional companies, referral services and headhunters.

If you're interested in attending a job fair, there are four types to consider:

1. **Industry**. These fairs are sponsored by a cross section of companies belonging to a particular industry, such as health care, food service, aerospace and the like.

2. **Skill or specialization**. These fairs are designed to attract candidates with a particular type of technical skill or specialized training. Typical skill fairs are sponsored by a wide range of companies whose common bond is their need for personnel in data processing, environmental management or engineering.

3. **Location**. Organized by the local chamber of commerce or other nonprofit organizations, these fairs are a great way of providing companies in your city with a pool of qualified candidates.

4. **Special group or affirmative action**. These fairs fulfill the needs of employers to interview candidates belonging to specific age, gender, or minority groups. An example is the annual Equal Employment Opportunity Career Expo of Southern Ohio, which acts as a magnet for minority candidates with software engineering or data processing experience.

A common concern among potential job fair attendees is confidentiality. For example, let's suppose your own company made plans to exhibit. How would you explain your presence at such a fair to your boss?

"The answer is simple," explains Bill Westerkamp, director of Career Expo in Cincinnati, Ohio. "We provide each candidate with a complete list of exhibitors in advance. For the candidate who feels uneasy about being seen in public, we'll set up a private, confidential interview with any company in attendance. That way, there's nothing to fear."

The informational interview

One of the best ways to learn what the job market's like (and what job openings might exist) is by talking with a key individual in your industry, or an authority who knows the lay of the land.

This type of conversation is called a *trial interview* or *informational interview*. Your goal should be to gather as much information as you can regarding your career options, without putting any pressure on yourself or the other person. All you want to do is hear the opinion of a knowledgeable professional, so the next time you interview, you're better prepared.

If the other person thinks you have promise, he or she will probably put you in touch with a contact who's a hiring manager. And, of course, you can always probe for leads during your meeting, so long as you do it tactfully, and with respect for the other person's kindness for spending time with you.

Here are some questions you might ask:

- Can you tell me about any trends you've noticed in our industry over the last few years?
- Can you make any comments on the way I present myself?
- Can you suggest any changes I might make that would improve my resume?
- Now that you know me better, can you think of any career direction that would particularly suit me? Why?
- Are there any companies that come to mind that would most appropriately fit my background and personality?
- Where do you see me 10 years from now?

89

So long as you let the person know in advance that their opinion is valuable to you, and that you're not necessarily asking for a job, an informational interview can be of enormous help to you—and may provide you with high-quality clues.

Go for the upgrade

So far, we've looked at ways to track down both advertised and unadvertised job openings. Now I'd like you to consider a different type of job opening—the one that doesn't exist.

What do I mean? Well, managers are sometimes receptive to the idea of adding a key person they feel would improve the quality of their staff, even if a formal job description hasn't been written. Recruiters call these hidden opportunities *upgrade* positions, which are created the instant the right candidate appears.

I've never been shy about alerting companies to the availability of talented candidates. In fact, many of the candidates I've placed have gone to work for employers that had no job openings.

Sheila is a perfect example. She got my name from someone I'd placed, and wanted me to help her find a job. I checked out her background, and found that she had a reputation as a sharp, highly motivated, well-rounded electrical engineer. So I decided to work with her.

Unfortunately, Sheila's specific skills were only loosely applicable to my clients' needs. What's more, she only had a couple of years' work experience. The only real selling point I could think of was her M.I.T. education, and the fact that she'd graduated with honors. I was hoping that would be enough.

One by one, I went through my list of clients—but no one was interested. Five days and a hundred phone calls later, I picked up a lead on a little electronics company in Marina Del Rey. Word had it they'd just landed a big, important contract with NASA. Surely, I thought, the company would need a bright electrical engineer like Sheila.

Since I didn't know anyone at the company, I decided to call the president, Dr. Zatzick. Why not start at the top?

"Dr. Zatzick, my name is Bill Radin, and I'm with an executive search firm here in Los Angeles. I'm calling to let you know about an extremely talented engineer who just came on the job market. Based on her past experience and educational credentials, I'm certain she'd be a tremendous asset to your company. Is this a good time to talk?"

"Bill, I appreciate your call, but I'm afraid we don't have any openings," Dr. Zatzick grumbled.

"Gee, that's too bad," I sighed. "It would be a shame for you not to talk to an honors graduate from M.I.T., especially since they're in such short supply."

"Wait. Did you say M.I.T.?" All of a sudden his tone lightened up.

"Yes, I did."

"Well, it might be a good idea for the two of us to get together. But like I said, we don't have any openings."

"I'll be sure to tell the candidate. By the way, you seem to feel strongly about M.I.T."

"That's right, I do. The best engineer I ever met went to school there, and helped me make this company what it is today. Maybe your candidate can work the same kind of magic."

"You never know. At the very least, you can spend some time with a sharp individual. How does tomorrow afternoon look for you?"

"That would be fine."

Sheila was hired on the spot the next day. The employer obviously felt her academic background would be an asset to his company, and would compensate for her lack of experience. The fact that she was hired, even though there was no opening, demonstrates the potential for landing a job that doesn't exist.

Increase your mileage—multitask your calls

The upgrade approach requires you to take the initiative and make things happen. Cold-calling an employer may not be the easiest task in the world, but I can guarantee you that you'll be rewarded by the effort you spend.

You may not land a new job from your very first phone call, but if you work smart, you should come away from each conversation with information that'll help you during the job-changing process.

The method of accumulating useful data from a single source is known to recruiters as *multitasking*. It doesn't take a rocket scientist to figure out that it's more efficient to extract five bits of information from one call than it is to make five different calls.

To help organize your method of information-gathering, let me share with you the five multitasking objectives you should shoot for the next time you call a prospective employer:

1. *Arrange an interview for yourself.* Set a time, date and place; and find out if there's anything special you should bring with you, or if there's anyone else you're likely to meet.

2. Once the interview is arranged, *probe for information* about the job and the people who'll interview you.

3. If you fail to line up an interview, *ask what's missing from your background,* and find out if the company's looking for any special skills. If you have these skills and you didn't have a chance to mention them before, repeat objective number one, and see if you can set up an interview.

4. *Find out all you can* about the company that may result in a match at a later date. Is it expanding? Adding a product line? Reorganizing? Implementing a new technology or methodology that's compatible with your expertise? Also, ask who its competitors are, and how they're different.

5. *Get referrals to other job openings at similar companies* if this one isn't interested. "Which companies in the local area would need a person with my background?" is an excellent question to ask. Once you get a referral, the next two questions should be, "Who do you suggest I talk to at the company?" and "What's that person's title?"

Take notes on 3 x 5 cards while you talk; or at the very least, write down the main points of your conversation after you've finished, and put them in a folder for future reference.

The beauty of multitasking is that the information you gather can be stored and used at a later date, along with all the job leads, articles, ads and referrals that might be relevant to your search. Like a good detective, you'll find that even the most insignificant "clues" might eventually crack the case.

Marketing tips: How to present your background

Earlier, I role-played a presentation for Andy York that you can use as a model to follow up on a classified ad response. But how would you construct an effective presentation if you were to cold-call a company, without knowing its hiring needs?

First, you'd need to make a concise list of your skills and accomplishments and, if you can, translate them into potential benefits to the target company. Imagine its needs, and the most likely way you could fill them. For example, if you have experience in desktop publishing using Macintosh computers, call every ad agency, publisher and large corporation that might circulate its own internal newsletter to see if they could use someone with your specialized skills.

Next, you'll want to construct a presentation or brief script that will spark the interest of the employer and create a dialogue. Here are some suggested openings:

"Mr. Employer, this is just an informational call."

"Let me explain the purpose of my call. I've got a solid background in our industry, and I'm exploring the job market."

"You and I have never met, but I wanted to speak with you regarding a confidential matter."

"I'm hoping you can help me, since you and I are both in the same industry."

"I need your advice regarding a career matter. Is this a good time to talk?"

Of course, you needn't duplicate my word patterns verbatim; you should use your own phraseology to describe your unique attributes and your interest in lending your expertise to a new employer. Listen carefully to what the other person has to say, and make sure to explore as much as possible the employer's needs. You may find that something in your background sparks an interest or pushes a hot button. As your conversation develops, work your way down the list of objectives we discussed earlier.

By presenting your background in this manner, you're putting into effect an educated guess that your skills are valuable to the employer. If you're correct, then you'll be asked to interview. If not, you'll have learned something about your marketability, and the company you called. In either case, you've expanded your network.

Finally, make sure you target your call within the company. I suggest you contact the hiring manager, or person in charge of making a decision. As a headhunter, I've learned that hiring managers, not personnel officials, usually make the best prospects.

The mail-order candidate

Another effective way to get your name and qualifications in front of prospective employers is to mail your resume *en masse*.

Using this technique, you can cover a larger territory in less time than calling each and every prospect; and you never have to face rejection personally. The drawback to mass mailing is that it's less personal than face-to-face (or voice-to-voice) contact; and as a result, your prospects will be less inclined to say "yes," or pass along any leads.

To compensate, you have to *increase the volume* of resumes mailed by developing a sizeable list of prospects. These can be arranged in the following categories:

1. **The hiring managers or contacts within target companies you already know.** These are obviously the most likely prospects. My approach would be to call them, rather than mail to them, but if you feel you communicate better on paper (or there are too many to call), then send your resume along with a cover letter directed to the person you know.

2. **Local companies that directly compete with yours, or employ people with similar skills.** This is the next best group, in that these companies are fairly easy to locate. Simply ask around to find out who they are, or look in the yellow pages or chamber of commerce directory, industrial guide or manufacturers register. If possible, get the name of the hiring manager, and address your envelope to his or her attention.

3. **Companies in a specific geographic location.** Let's say you want to move to Kansas City. First, call the Kansas City Chamber of Commerce, and ask for help in locating companies that employ people within your industry or area of expertise. Next, you'll need to spend some time in the library, browsing through the Kansas City yellow pages. See if you can locate a directory of businesses in the Kansas City area. You might also check with your trade association, and get a membership listing by location. Finally, look for publications that provide geographic compilations of specific products or services, such as *The World Aerospace Directory* or *The Fluid Power Handbook.*

4. **Any company that might hire someone with your background.** This will become your largest list, and to help you manage it, I suggest you tap into the resources available to professional direct marketers. For example, you might want to call a list broker or direct marketing company, who will charge you by the number of names you either rent or buy. (Rented lists can only be used once or twice, and therefore, they're less expensive.) The highest-quality list is one that's "clean," or recently updated, and includes a specific contact name, such as "Ron Boustead, Data Processing Manager," rather than just "MIS Director."

When mailing your resumes, mark the envelopes "Personal and Confidential," and address them to the hiring manager or personnel director. It's preferable to type or laser print each envelope, since letters with stick-on labels resemble junk mail, and they'll more than likely get thrown away. Likewise, it's a good idea to avoid using postal imprints or meter tape for postage—first-class stamps add a more personal touch.

If you know you're going to be moving to or visiting a specific area, you can write a brief cover letter outlining your itinerary, or simply attach a post-it note on your resume that says something like: "I will be interviewing in Kansas City the week of February 12. Please contact me to arrange a time."

Live better electronically

Electronic databases can also be used to help you compile a list of prospective employers. If you have a home computer, services like CompuServe will enable you to gain access to thousands of bits of relevant information. Or, you can simply go to the library and ask them to run a search of possible employers from their system.

Using a database gives you an incredible degree of thoroughness and flexibility. Not only can you scan through the thousands of companies listed under the Standard Industrial Classification (or SIC code), a database lets you sift through the information you retrieve, and sort for company size, zip code, and so forth. This way, you can maximize your selectivity and creativity when targeting a new company.

Another marvelous feature of a database is its potential for specificity. I recently ran a survey of all companies in the United States that manufactured motors and generators. I found that there were 1,118 companies listed under the SIC 3821 category. Then, by tapping into the Dun & Bradstreet "SIC 2+2" database, I broke down the SIC 3821 classification into 33 very specialized subclasses, including "industrial armatures," "coils," "collector rings," "synchronous condensers," "frequency converters" and so on. I was astounded by how specific I could get, and by the way this type of information lends itself to direct marketing.

By matching specific product groups with zip codes, company size and the names of key managers, you'll be able to focus your search as narrowly or broadly as you want.

The power of persistence

As in any self-improvement endeavor, you'll find your own persistence to be your greatest ally. This is especially true when it comes to pursuing "filled" positions.

Many people make the mistake of assuming that after an offer's been extended to or accepted by another candidate, the deal's in the bag. The saying goes, it's not over 'til it's over.

Let me encourage you by saying that several times a year, I place candidates into positions that were already "filled." Here are seven good reasons to keep your hopes alive:

1. **The turndown.** This is when the primary candidate decides not to take the job you want. The phrase, "I'll think it over," is often just a euphemism for, "I don't have the heart to tell you I'm not really interested." As a headhunter, those four words ("I'll think it over") make me more worried than a golfer in a thunderstorm—unless they're uttered by a candidate other than my own.

2. **The counteroffer.** This is a leverage tactic used by a candidate who accepts the job, then turns around and uses the offer as a way to leverage a raise out of his or her present company. This turn of events often results in an unfilled position, and an opportunity for you.

3. **The delayed counteroffer.** This is when a counteroffer is accepted after a candidate starts work with a new company.

   For example, I placed a candidate who went to work for my client company, cashed his sign-on bonus check, then quit after one week. Where did he end up? Back at his old job. It seems his old boss called him every evening at home during his brief tenure with the new employer, and tempted him back to the old company with a big promotion.

4. **The no-show.** This is also called *candidate evaporation* by recruiters. Usually, an eleventh-hour revelation strikes the candidate like a thunderbolt, and he never shows up his first day of work. This leaves the

new employer feeling like a jilted bride at the wedding altar; but the no-show creates a golden opportunity for you.

5. **The job that didn't work out.** This occurs when the candidate and employer realize they made an honest mistake, and abort the mission. Even the most experienced professional will bail out quickly in such a situation, and get on with his or her life.

6. **The failed drug test or physical.** This usually happens a few days before the primary candidate starts work, and gives you the chance to waltz into a new position (assuming you can pass the test).

   Sometimes, an error can complicate the drug screening process. For instance, Bernie, a candidate of mine, accepted a position with one of my clients. After his physical exam, he was told he tested positive for opiates (which are found in cocaine), and the offer would have to be withdrawn.

   This doesn't make sense, Bernie thought. Later, he realized the problem—he'd been taking pain medication he'd purchased over the counter in his native Ireland. Thinking quickly, he flattened the box the pills came in, and faxed the image to the testing lab. Since pain-killers containing opiates are perfectly legal in Ireland, the company waived Bernie's physical examination, and the offer stood.

   However, the results from a failed drug test or physical exam usually hold up, creating a situation that will breathe new life into your candidacy.

7. **The fatal background check.** This is when a company can't verify a candidate's past employment, salary, degree, citizenship status, credit history or security clearance. Too often, a background check isn't completed until after a candidate starts a new job; and the results invalidate the company's offer of employment.

   I worked with a candidate once whose offer from a major corporation was withdrawn after the company found out the candidate's brother was a convicted drug dealer.

Because of the unpredictable nature of the hiring process, it makes sense to follow up every job lead, even if you're told the deal's already done, and the other candidate has either accepted an offer or started a new job. A perfectly reasonable question to ask a hiring manager is, "When will the new person start?" or, "I just wanted to follow up to see if you'll keep my name under consideration, should things not work out with the new candidate—may I call you back in a month?" Make sure to mark the date on your calendar, and stay in touch. You never know when you might suddenly change from a dark horse to a front runner.

> *By using every resource available, you'll increase your odds of getting the job you want.*

7 Corporate Headhunters: Your Job-Search Commandos

Corporate headhunters (also known as executive recruiters or executive search consultants) have firmly established themselves as a visible and highly valued fixture in today's employment landscape. Through their aggressive matchmaking, headhunters affect the careers of individuals, the lives of their families and friends, and the profitability of entire corporations.

No one knows exactly what the business world would be like without the influence of headhunters, but one thing's for sure: sometime in your career, you'll either receive a call from a headhunter, or initiate contact yourself. In either case, you should learn how to work with them effectively, and take full advantage of the many benefits their service provides.

Naturally, my perspective on the executive search business is a bit *slanted*. Those of us in the profession realize we're neither saints nor miracle workers; however, there are clearly many advantages to developing a good working relationship with a corporate headhunter:

- **Greater exposure.** Headhunters not only maintain a myriad of existing contacts within your field, they can also scout out new companies you never heard of.

- **Increased efficiency.** Headhunters are obsessive networkers; they spend their time researching and penetrating the employment market. Their knowledge of your industry can save you time in identifying and pursuing prospective employers.
- **Personalized public relations.** Employers generally look more favorably at a candidate who's professionally recommended. Headhunters stake their reputations on the quality of their candidates, and will always present you in the best possible light.
- **Confidential representation.** Some job search situations require a great deal of discretion. For example, you may want to explore an opportunity with your present company's direct competitor. In such an instance, a headhunter can present your background confidentially, thereby protecting your identity, and eliminating (or at least minimizing) your risk of exposure.
- **Authoritative career consulting.** Headhunters can help you determine the job or career track that's right for you, based on current market conditions and your own values and abilities. They're also in a unique position to walk you through (and monitor) each step in your job changing process.
- **Private training.** Headhunters can give you practical, time-tested suggestions on how to strengthen your resume and improve your interviewing technique. In many ways, a headhunter acts as a personal coach.
- **Third-party representation.** As experienced brokers, headhunters find ways to put favorable deals together, and iron out differences you and the hiring company may have regarding your salary, benefits and relocation package.

In addition, working through a headhunter can actually improve your chances for success once you've been placed. That's because the search fee the hiring company paid the recruiter represents a sizable financial investment in your future success—an investment worth protecting.

The missing link

Headhunting is a multibillion-dollar international industry that acts as the missing link between a half-million job seekers and employers each year. At last count, there were more than 125,000 executive search practitioners in the United States, according to *The Fordyce Letter*, the industry's leading trade journal.

There's hardly an industry or profession that hasn't spawned its own coterie of recruiters. They cover every conceivable pocket of the job market, from food sales to machine design to motion picture financing to mortgage banking to freight hauling to data communications to haute cuisine to college administration to city management.

Generally speaking, headhunters work within well-defined niches. To make sense of a complicated employment market, headhunters classify their candidates according to:

- **Title or function,** which refers to their descriptive title or rank within the company, such as president, plant manager, staff accountant, director of nursing, and so on.
- **Skill or application,** which refers to their specialized abilities, such as tax accounting, IBM AS/400 systems programming, secured lending, and the like.
- **Product or service,** which refers to the industry in which the candidates do their work, such as plastics, minicomputers, industrial tools, public administration, hospitality, and so forth.

To give you an example, a recruiter might place project engineers (title) with computer-aided design experience (skill) into positions with companies that built submarine hydraulic systems (product).

Other headhunters might place CEOs (title) with plant management experience (skill) who work for companies that process frozen broccoli (product); or district sales managers (title) with marketing degrees (skill) who work for companies that make high-top leather sneakers (product).

Think of your own experience. How would you classify yourself? Your answer will not only help you put your career into perspective; it'll help the headhunter determine whether you "fit" into his or her market niche.

Of course, recruiters can use other means to define their markets. Some take an *industry-specific* approach. Let's say you work in the retail industry, or in construction. You'll probably find a recruiter who doesn't care what your title or function is, as long as you have experience in that target market. I knew a recruiter named Jim, who specialized in the printing industry. No matter what you did in the past, if it had anything to do with printing, Jim would take you under his wing.

The opposite approach is taken by the *skill-specific* recruiters. To them, the product or service of the host company is secondary to the skills of their candidates. This is the preferred method of recruiters who specialize in placement of data processing, accounting or clerical personnel.

Don't get lost in the shuffle

Even though headhunters can't guarantee you a new job, you have much to gain from working with them. And vice-versa, since you represent an addition to their continuously perishable inventory. While it's true that headhunters owe their allegiance to their client companies (who pay the fees), without candidates to fuel the fire, headhunters simply wouldn't exist.

For each search assignment, headhunters may *prescreen* hundreds of prospects. Therefore, the majority of their time is spent with the finalists for each open position, relegating to their file drawers the "reject" or the "maybe next time" candidates they encounter. These candidates are often highly skilled professionals who simply don't fit the specific qualifications required by the headhunter's client company—they're simply in the wrong place at the wrong time.

For that reason, you should always press for a realistic appraisal of your chances of being placed. If one isn't forthcoming, you can assume the recruiter is giving your candidacy a low priority. In that case, you can opt to let your resume languish in a headhunter's file, or seek the help of a recruiter who'll take an active role in finding you a new position.

I try my best to be up-front with every candidate I talk to. If your skills fall outside my area of expertise, I'll steer you to another headhunter who can be of assistance, or provide you with some general coaching that I hope will be of value.

Always look for a headhunter who takes an interest in your background, or who specializes in your industry. The last thing you need is to pin your hopes on someone who's not in a position to help you. Be prepared for mixed reviews when you talk to recruiters. You might very well receive a brush-off like, "I'll call you in a week to 10 days"; or bad advice, such as "You'll never find the job you want with the background you have"; or discouragement like, "Nobody's hiring now." Just keep plugging away at your job search—and never take "No" from a headhunter.

Of course, even the most qualified candidacy is subject to the whims of a supply-and-demand job market. In many cases, a headhunter simply won't know what your chances of getting another job might be until he or she puts out feelers or sends you out on an interview. To work most efficiently, invest your time with a recruiter who really wants to help you.

Sigmund, Sherlock, and Donald

Headhunters come from a wide variety of backgrounds, and exhibit the same range of personal merits and character strengths as the rest of the human race. The majority are honest, hardworking entrepreneurs, who work diligently to help candidates find meaningful, rewarding jobs.

I've found that headhunters can be divided into three different personality types:

1. The **Sigmund Freud** headhunter is a kindly, wise and empathic counselor. He or she listens carefully when you describe your values, your job preferences, your personal goals and your family commitments.

The Sigmund Freud headhunter wants to place you with a company you'll feel comfortable working for, and will spend lots of time getting to know you.

2. The **Sherlock Holmes** headhunter is a clever, relentless, goal-oriented detective, who'll track down and contact every company that might provide a match for your skills. This type can be quite creative in discovering aspects of your background that can be successfully marketed to companies off the beaten track, or only peripherally related to your present industry.

   A perfect example of the Sherlock Holmes headhunter is Norman Roberts, who works in Los Angeles. It was his ingenuity that led to an unlikely (but highly successful) match in 1984. He took an unknown travel industry executive, Peter Ueberroth, and placed him as the head of the U.S. Olympic committee.

3. The **Donald Trump** headhunter is the consummate deal maker. This type is less concerned with whether you're a round or square peg, as long as you can be crunched into whatever hole may be available or convenient. Headhunters like this tend to give the search industry a bad name because of their insensitivity to the true needs of their clients and candidates; and although they can often produce positive results, many times their high-pressure tactics lead to short-term employment.

While personality and style are important aspects to consider when selecting a headhunter, you should also evaluate the headhunter's *past results*. Assuming you feel a modicum of comfort with the person you're dealing with, it's a good idea to check into his or her track record and experience level. If you discover a consistent pattern of success, you're probably off to a good start.

Otherwise, you might find yourself stuck with the fourth type of headhunter: the *Inspector Clouseau*. This type embodies none of the above personality traits, only the endearing, bumbling incompetence of the movie character portrayed by the late Peter Sellers. In his *Pink Panther* movies, Inspector Clouseau was able to crack the trickiest cases; but only through sheer serendipity or plain dumb luck.

The two-party system

You've probably heard of the so-called schism in the world of executive search between "retained" and "contingency" headhunters. True, differences exist, especially in regard to billing methods, candidate salary levels, and operational procedures.

However, I prefer to think of the entire search industry as a microcosm of the American political system, in which both Republicans and Democrats live in peaceful coexistence.

"Gee, that's a far-fetched analogy, isn't it?" you ask.

No, not really. Republicans and Democrats are both loyal Americans; they just have different views concerning society and the way the country should be run.

The same could be said of the retained recruiters (who get their fees paid in advance and work to fill higher-level positions) and the contingency folks (who only get paid once their candidates are hired). Each serves a different slice of the employment population, and each has a different concept of how the search business should work.

Interestingly, the lines of demarcation have begun to blur in recent years. Just as Republicans and Democrats have cross-bred portions of their constituencies, so have the retained and contingency headhunters. Although the traditional break point in salary is around $75,000 (with retained above and contingency below) it's no longer unheard of for a contingency recruiter to place a CEO at $200,000 a year; or a retained headhunter to place a manufacturing manager at $55,000. What's more, each camp will, if the situation warrants, borrow from the other's method of billing the client. Lately, I've heard stories of contingency recruiters charging partially retained fees, and retainer headhunters accepting assignments "on spec."

As the search industry continues to evolve, it'll matter less how the client is billed. Currently, there are about a dozen different billing schemes, from flat fees to hourly fees to itemized service charges. One clever recipe combines contingency with retained to produce—*voilà!*—"contained" search.

Understanding these broad divisions will help avoid confusion and save you time if your salary level is fairly polarized. That is, if you're currently earning, say, $35,000, there's virtually no chance you'll be working any time soon with a retained headhunter. Similarly, if you're earning more than $100,000, the odds are, the headhunter you work with will be retained by the client company.

Both contingency and retained recruiters play for big stakes. Fees generally run from 20 percent to as high as 35 percent of a placed candidate's first-year compensation. With that type of arithmetic, it's easy to see why headhunters develop ulcers, not to mention a healthy skepticism toward their clients and candidates. All it takes is for an employer or candidate to change his mind at the last minute, and the headhunter has lost, say, $10,000 or $20,000 in personal income for months of work.

Of greater concern

Lately, a new controversy has begun to rage within the executive search community. It has nothing to do with how a client is billed; the dispute centers on the issue of *candidate marketing*.

Some headhunters feel it's inappropriate to pick up the phone and "sell" a highly qualified candidate to an employer who isn't necessarily looking to hire anyone. The marketing *refuseniks* cite the employer's perception of "conflict of interest" as the reason, since the headhunter is sworn to serve only the needs of the client company. In such a case, wouldn't the introduction of an unsolicited candidate muddy the waters?

Not at all, say the advocates of candidate marketing (of which I'm one). They feel they're simply helping an individual improve his or her life, while at the same time strengthening the staff of a deserving company.

While it's statistically unlikely that any given headhunter will immediately clear his desk to mount a concerted job campaign on your behalf, that possibility always exists—if you work with someone who's open to candidate marketing.

Your relationship with a headhunter can vary from a periodic conversation—"Let's stay in touch if something comes up"—to an intense, energetic "I'm gonna work like the devil on your behalf" job search. Most headhunters will keep you on file until there's a need for your services; relatively few will actively scan the market.

My goal has always been to put good candidates and good companies together. If I think that goal can be accomplished through candidate marketing, I'll give it a try, especially if the candidate has unique skills in my area of specialization, or is in some way extraordinary.

The Ivy League quarterback

A few years ago, when I worked in Los Angeles, I took a call from Dalton, an entry-level candidate.

It seems he'd been recruited by a large aerospace company while in his senior year in college. They'd offered him an engineering position, which, they said, would be waiting for him in L.A. as soon as he finished school.

After graduation, Dalton had packed his bags and moved from New Hampshire to California. His first day on the job, the company told him they were sorry, but the defense budget was recently slashed, and his position had been eliminated.

Could I help him find a job?

This may sound crazy, but somehow, I *knew* I could place this candidate, so I asked him to come into my office for a chat.

Here he was, an unsolicited 21-year-old kid from another coast with a degree in mechanical engineering and no work experience outside of college. Not much to work with, right?

Wrong.

The moment he walked into my office, I knew from his rugged good looks, impeccable attire and self-assured demeanor that he was someone very special. His warm greeting and firm handshake immediately broke the ice, and I motioned to him to have a seat.

"So, Dalton, where did you go to college?" I asked.

"An Ivy League school in New England called Dartmouth," Dalton replied.

"Do anything special there?"

"Well, I did play a couple years of varsity football."

"No kidding. What position?" I asked.

"Oh, quarterback."

"That's nice," I said. "What can you tell me about school? Any particular interests?"

"Well, I spent a considerable amount of time as a work-study student in the sports medicine lab, doing biomechanical research using college athletes as subjects," Dalton told me. "In fact, my senior thesis was based on our findings. The aerospace company that brought me out here to L.A. wanted me to work on the space shuttle program, concentrating on ergonomics research." Dalton paused, and looked me right in the eye. "Do you think you can help me find a job?"

"I don't know," I said, although I was beginning to feel he was pretty placeable. "Any other special interests you can tell me about?"

"Well, I didn't have much time for outside activities, other than my academic honor society. You see, I was pretty busy working five nights a week as a bartender to put myself through school," he said.

OK, I had heard enough! By this point, I knew that placing him with a company was only a matter of how quickly I could dial a telephone. In fact, I felt like I could send him on an interview with my invoice pinned to his jacket! What employer wouldn't want an intelligent, hard-working piece of gold like Dalton?

After I walked him to the door and thanked him for coming in, I literally ran back to my desk and furiously began dialing.

First call: the UCLA mechanical engineering department. Did they know of any companies doing biomechanical research in the Los Angeles area?

Well, yes. There's a little company out in Woodland Hills called Biomedical Analysis Associates.

Great. Did they happen to have the number? Fine.

Second call: Hi, is this BAA? Who's your company president? Oh, he's the only full-time employee aside from the receptionist? That's OK. Would you connect me, please? Thank you. Hello, Mr. Employer, this is Bill Radin, and I work for an executive search firm in Los Angeles. You wouldn't believe who I just met...

Get the edge you deserve

Well, you can probably guess the rest of the story. The interview took place the next morning. By noon, the company president and I had hammered out a deal, and Dalton started his new job the following Monday.

The decision whether to market a candidate, and under what conditions, is obviously left to the discretion of each headhunter. I used to work with another recruiter who would get two or three calls a day from entry-level candidates. His response never varied. In a tone designed to let them know how much they were wasting his time, he told them, sorry, I can't help you if you don't have experience. Call me back in a couple of years.

I hate to think of all the candidates my associate could have helped (and all the fees he would have collected) had he broadened his constituency a little. Don't misunderstand me; I'm not confusing headhunters with social workers. The old saying, "Our stock in trade is the obvious," didn't become the headhunter's creed by accident.

But if you look hard enough (and you want results right away), you may be able to find a recruiter who'll take a special interest in your career. The right headhunter can give you a competitive edge in more ways than you can imagine.

Narrowing the field

To find a headhunter who'll serve your needs (assuming one hasn't already found *you*), ask for a confidential recommendation from a friend or professional associate in your field. Or, you can always look in the local yellow pages under "employment." If you need to, go to the library and sift through *The Directory of Executive Recruiters,* which is categorized by discipline and divided into retainer and contingency sections; or scan *The National Directory of Personnel Consultants.*

The first thing you'll want to do once you find a search firm is find out if its specialty is compatible with your background. For example, the Sales Consultants franchise has a national reputation for excellence, but their recruiters only work with sales and marketing professionals. It would do you no good to register with sales consultants if your background is in hospital administration or yogurt manufacturing.

Next, find out if the firm's geographic capability suits your needs. If you live in Cedar Rapids and want to relocate to Denver, see if your local firm has clients in the Denver market, or can recommend other recruiters in that area.

Once you select a local company, make an appointment with one of the recruiters on staff. You should expect to spend an hour or so in their office. Many firms will ask you to fill out an application or data sheet while you wait, so be prepared to list former employers, references, and the like. Also bring a clean copy of your resume, and by all means, dress and act as though you were on a formal employment interview. The way you handle yourself with a recruiter will reveal your degree of professionalism, and will very likely affect the recruiter's level of enthusiasm for working with you.

Answer all questions as honestly and completely as you can, especially when it comes to your timetable for changing jobs. Headhunters hate to "hurry up and wait," or try to second-guess the people they want to help. If you're not serious about making a change, don't waste the recruiter's time.

Multiple registration means greater exposure

Another way to find a job in a new city (or increase your overall exposure) is to register with a firm that's part of a national organization, or belongs to a recruiting network. Simply ask if your background information can be entered into its internal system. Once you're in, your name will be added to a large database, thereby maximizing your chances of getting placed.

Contingency firms such as Management Recruiters, Dunhill, Sanford Rose, and Snelling Personnel Services operate in hundreds of locations, and usually cross over into countless disciplines. Skill-specific firms, who concentrate on placing accounting, clerical, and data processing personnel, are also quite ubiquitous. Robert Half, Adia, and Source EDP are some of the more prominent players is this field.

Less numerous are the industry-specific organizations like Retail Recruiters and Healthcare Recruiters. Their branch offices usually can be found in the larger metropolitan areas. If you cross into the realm of the retained recruiter, there are several well-known, established search firms to turn to, such as Korn/Ferry, Russell Reynolds, Spencer Stuart, and Heidrick & Struggles.

An increasing number of firms, both large and small, belong to national networks, which share current candidate lists and job opening information. One of the largest is Inter-city Personnel Associates, a *generalist* network headquartered in Appleton, Wis. Its 240 subscribers use the network to increase their coverage, and to "split" deals within their membership.

Additional organizations, such as National Computer Associates, The National Banking Network, The National Association of Physician Recruiters and The National Environmental Network, act as independent employment hotlines, connecting skill-specific candidates with the appropriate client companies.

Some common-sense ground rules

Let's talk turkey for a minute about what to expect from headhunters, and how to establish some common-sense ground rules. Here are seven issues you'll want to discuss before you set any relationship in stone:

1. **Compatibility.** Make sure you feel comfortable with the style, personality, intensity level and integrity of the headhunter. As in any other business relationship, you want the other person to understand your needs and act accordingly.

2. **Confidentiality.** Make sure your resume isn't going to get plastered all over town without your knowledge. An inept (or anxious) recruiter can overexpose your candidacy; or, worse, reveal your intention to change jobs to your own company.

3. **Good judgment.** Make sure you're being sent to interviews that match your background and interests with the needs of the recruiter's client company.

The most common complaint from both candidates and employers is that recruiters "throw candidates against the wall to see what sticks."

4. **Honesty.** Make sure there's either a *bona fide* job opening or an upgrade possibility where you're being sent to interview. Otherwise, you'll be spending your valuable time on one wild goose chase after another.

5. **Velocity.** Make sure to let the recruiter know at what pace you want to proceed in your search for a new position. If you're not ready to make a change until a later date, or simply want to explore the market, don't let the recruiter waste your time by sending you on an interview.

6. **Arm-twisting.** Don't be pressured into accepting a position or a compensation package simply to please the recruiter.

7. **Exclusivity.** It's fine to work with a recruiter on an exclusive basis, as long as you feel comfortable with the arrangement, and the recruiter has earned the right of sole representation. On the other hand, you might not want to limit your options. Despite what you may be told, no recruiter has the exclusive "ownership" of your candidacy.

By the same token, you must be fair with headhunters. For example, if you're pursuing a job search on your own or through another party, keep the headhunter aware of your activity, so you don't cross paths. A recruiter's time and reputation are his most valuable commodities; he or she deserves better than to be manipulated or left in the lurch.

It works both ways

Finally, level with whoever you're working with. I almost called the fire department one day when I smelled something burning in the rest room down the hall from my office. It turned out one of my colleagues' candidates had lied to him about his salary, and after my colleague found out, he decided to file the candidate's resume using the *incendiary* system.

114

More than once I've had to explain to a candidate that it's unethical for me to falsely represent his salary or achievements. If you're earning $53,750 annually, that's exactly what I'll tell the employer. Otherwise, I'd be inflating your salary as a negotiating ploy, which makes me very uncomfortable. I prefer to think of myself as a headhunter, not a camel trader.

Recruiters can't work miracles by waving a magic wand over your resume; all they can do is match your background with a suitable opening, and help guide you through the job-changing process efficiently and competitively.

> *It makes good sense to build a solid relationship with a corporate headhunter.*

8 Hired Guns: The Third-Party Specialists

Headhunters aren't the only types of career advisers who can give your job search a boost. For a fee, you can tap into the products and services of the hired guns, the third-party specialists who offer their clients everything from resume consultation to psychological testing to audio cassette self-help programs to career counseling.

The hired guns will make one thing very clear up front: They can't guarantee you an interview or a new job as a result of using the products or services they sell. So it's particularly important to evaluate whether your money will be wisely invested, especially when the dollars start flying.

Paying someone to perform a service in which the results aren't guaranteed can be a pretty scary proposition. It reminds me of the horrible mistake I made once when I signed up with a video dating service. Although the company I worked with was careful not to make any promises when I plunked down the big bucks, they didn't hesitate to hard-sell me on the likelihood of a hot romance or a long-term relationship. As if to prove the effectiveness of their brokerage, I was presented with a long list of satisfied customers who'd fallen in love and gotten married.

Though I was well aware that nothing was guaranteed, I still spent $1,600 on their service—and never went on a single date. Hopefully, your investment in the service of a hired gun will yield a greater return than mine.

Your resume options: Economy or deluxe

Take a close look at your resume. If it's already getting you positive results, fine; don't fix it. However, if you feel it could use some improvement in its appearance, or you need to make minor changes in its content, then pay a visit to your neighborhood quick-print shop, for a high-quality job at an affordable price.

Most of the well-known franchised quick-print outfits like PIP or Kinko's can photocopy your resume on the proper paper if you hand them the camera-ready master copy; or typeset and edit a rough draft to give it a more professional appearance. Many quick-print stores also offer hourly computer rentals. For a small fee, you can sit behind a Macintosh or personal computer in the store and format your resume using a special software package or word-processing program. Once you've written what you want, you can then run several copies on the laser printer, or photocopy whatever amount you need.

If you're unsure about the appearance, quality or effectiveness of your resume, it might be a good idea to visit a resume consultant for a tune-up or, if necessary, a complete overhaul. Most will charge an hourly fee of between $35 and $75 (some go as high as $150 per hour); the rest will sell their expertise on a per-service basis. It certainly can't hurt to get a second opinion from a resume consultant; and having a professional wordsmith rework anything from a single phrase to the entire document will help create a more powerful impression in the mind of the reader.

Even if the resume service does nothing more than correct a typo or spelling error, the fee you've paid will have been wisely spent. Since more and more companies judge candidates by the quality of their written communication skills, the last thing you want is to be denied an interview opportunity or job offer because of an imperfect or poorly written resume.

Here's a case in point: Recently, I received a neatly typed resume from an extremely capable engineer. Despite the fact that he's an educated person (who holds a bachelor's degree in electrical engineering and a master's in business administration), he managed to misspell the words *develop* ("develope") and *laid* ("layed"). Sure, we all make mistakes. But suppose you were an employer, and you were considering this candidate for a $60,000 a year managerial position. Would you let these errors influence your hiring decision? In today's competitive market, you probably would.

Some real-life examples

Barbara Kordis of Cincinnati, Ohio, runs a resume service called Professional Profile. Her clients depend on her to help them accurately (and forcefully) communicate their accomplishments via the written page. Some of the candidates she works with have been employed by the same company for 20 or 30 years, and have little experience when it comes to putting together a resume. They either find it difficult to explain what they've done in their careers, or they're too modest to "blow their own horns" by describing in detail their professional contributions or achievements. For these types of clients, Barbara conducts thorough interviews to collect the data she needs to construct entire resumes from scratch.

For her clients with existing resumes, Barbara performs a kind of paper-and-ink surgery to improve their resumes' appearance and content. To do this, she takes poorly written or awkward phrases and transforms them into clear, powerful statements of fact.

In the following examples, notice the difference between the original and revised phrases as Barbara:

- *Simplifies the meaning:*

Original: Maintained 100% of monthly sales goals even though the economy has caused significant reduction in company revenues.

Revised: Consistently achieved 100% of quota during a downturn in business and economy.

• *Restrains the tendency to editorialize:*

Original: Collected thousands of dollars in overdue billing by appealing to clients' integrity and persuading them to adhere to a payment time frame.

Revised: Collected thousands of dollars in receivables through proactive collection procedures while maintaining positive customer rapport.

• *Improves the syntax:*

Original: Developed sales information sheet for clients who sell our services, which has increased service and sales.

Revised: Increased sales and service by developing a sales information guide for clients.

• *Reduces verbosity:*

Original: Uncovered a client's questionable practices that were causing a $400-$1,000 loss in company revenues monthly. Reported the discovery, described the practices, detailed the consequences, and made recommendations to avoid the loss. The company accepted my recommendations and has avoided the loss.

Revised: Saved $12,000 annually by implementing new procedures on rental of equipment.

• *Softens the braggadocio:*

Original: Won more letters of praise from clients than anyone else in company history.

Revised: Consistently recognized by clients for excellent service.

Since your resume's format, style, grammar, spelling, syntax and accuracy are important in today's employment market, you'll want to choose a resume service very carefully. I've seen candidates pay good money only to end up with resumes that were worse than what they started with. Ask the service for references and examples of their work; and be sure to check to see what types of clients use the service you're considering, to see if your counselor has experience using the jargon and technical terminology germane to your industry.

Add-on nauseam

Many resume services offer far more than just resumes. A quick glance in the yellow pages under "Resumes" will reveal a menagerie of add-on products and services available to the job seeker, including "personal marketing packages," "presentation folders," "job-search and interview training," "career counseling," and so on.

In addition to offering a standard resume and cover letter package for a $75 to $275 minimum fee, a typical "full-service" resume shop might also encourage you to purchase some nifty (and costly) add-ons, such as:

- A **personnel profile test** ($125) to help you determine your personal and professional interests, aptitudes, strengths and weaknesses.

- A **job-search notebook** ($69) to organize and track your job-hunting activities.

- An **interview guide** ($30), which includes a workbook and audiotape program.

- A **mailing service** ($5 per letter) in case you don't have the time to follow up on job leads or mail your own resume.

- A **correspondence service** ($25 per service) for generating follow-up letters (such as, "Dear Sir/Madam: I sent you my resume three weeks ago, and haven't heard a thing..."), reference sheets, salary history addenda and thank-you letters.

- An entry into an **electronic resume listing service** ($15 to $20 per page), which serves an on-line network of subscribing companies.

Other resume services offer videotaped practice interviews, group motivational meetings, crash courses in networking techniques, and personal career counseling. If these add-ons are what you need, and you can afford to fly first-class, fine. Just be sure you don't get talked into an extra $300 or $400 worth of self-help bells and whistles that are either extraneous or can be obtained for less from other sources.

Getting exactly what you need

The increasing demand for more sophisticated and personalized job-seeking tools has spawned a veritable cottage industry of third-party specialists. A perfect example of this new breed of consultants is Dr. Tim Serey, a professor of management and organizational behavior at Northern Kentucky University. His company, Upward Careers, provides many of the standard services found in the resume preparation industry, plus a few value-added extras.

In addition to resume writing, counseling and testing, Tim will actually help you *prepare* for any interview you arrange by providing you with the target company's corporate biography, current company financial data, and a corporate competitive analysis, courtesy of the Dow Jones News Retrieval Service.

Tim's professional and academic credentials distinguish him from a crowded field in an unregulated industry. His goal is to custom-design a package of services based on your specific needs.

Market research is another service offered by third-party specialists. While it's true that most sources of information are available for free at your local library, many candidates lack the time or training to accurately compile a list of target companies. If you need personalized assistance (and you're willing to pay the price), you can get help from independent researchers. Known as *infopreneurs*, these professional data diggers can quickly find the information you need from a variety of sources, mostly electronic. Fees range from $50 to $100 per hour, with turnaround time within a few days. Infopreneurs will only retrieve the data you ask for, and won't bog you down with unnecessary information.

Electronic listing services

How would you like your resume or skill summary to be available to thousands of decision-makers? Well, through the miracle of computers, you can pay a flat fee to be entered into an electronic listing service, accessible to subscribing companies.

One such service is offered by Peterson's Connexion of Princeton, N.J. For a $40 annual application fee (but free to currently enrolled students), you can have your background distilled into education and skill codes, and plopped onto a database. The only requirement is that you possess a four-year degree from an accredited college or university.

Originally designed as a means for companies to locate graduating seniors through college placement offices, the Connexion file has grown to include 50,000 entry-level and experienced job-seekers. Subscribing companies nationwide (more than 200 at last count) can access the database directly through Peterson's in order to search for qualified candidates. As an added feature, Peterson's protects the privacy of its registered candidates by limiting the access of their list to subscribing companies. That means your name won't be traded off indiscriminately to third parties or sold to mail-order houses.

Another listing service, Resumes On Line, concentrates on local markets. For example, if you live in the New York City metropolitan area, you can join the other 5,000 candidates whose resumes are available to companies on a per-use basis.

The drawback to these types of services is that you never know who will be looking at your resume, or how often. Just because a company subscribes to an electronic listing service won't guarantee that they'll actually use the service with any regularity or intensity. Critics of listing services argue that many of the subscribing companies either fail to take full advantage of the database offerings or don't know how to properly access the information available. And if you happen to have a skill that's highly defined, off the beaten track, or non-transferable, your odds of hitting the right company will be pretty slim.

While the number of candidates using these services continues to rise, the actual percentage of placements currently being made as a result of electronic listings remains relatively small. However, when you consider the big payoff from the investment in this "lottery" style approach, you can see why these services have become so popular, especially in niche markets, such as civil service, corporate planning, or nonprofit organizational management.

Additional support from the outplacement professionals

Outplacement firms offer a dazzling array of services to the unemployed job seeker. Generally, these firms will only assist the terminated candidates of client companies, who pay the outplacement firms large fees in an effort to find their displaced personnel new employment (and assuage their own guilt for having laid them off in the first place).

However, some *retail* outplacement firms will (for a fairly hefty fee) accept individual clients who are interested in making use of the many services available, such as career testing, resume construction, individual counseling, market research, letter-generating, interviewing role-playing, and so forth.

Especially attractive to unemployed candidates are the "administrative services" most outplacement firms offer, in the form of private office space, telephones and secretarial support. Having these services at your disposal can be advantageous for a number of reasons.

- **Continuity**. Commuting to an office each morning can help you maintain your self-image as an employed professional, and prevent boredom or discouragement.
- **Motivation**. Working in an office environment with other professionals will help you sustain your focus on getting another job, and provide you with an atmosphere of optimism and moral support.

- **Camaraderie.** Sharing your experiences with a counselor or with other clients is a good way to preserve your level of confidence and self-esteem.
- **Convenience.** Having a typewriter, word processor, copy machine and fax machine at your disposal can save you time and reduce frustration.
- **Public image.** Presenting yourself as employed or professionally represented will elevate your stature in the eyes of prospective employers. The receptionist's telephone greeting, "Good morning. Executive offices; may I help you?" projects a much more professional image than answering the phone at home, or relying on a roommate, spouse or answering machine to take your calls during business hours.

As hired guns, outplacement firms make no guarantees that the services they provide will lead directly to an interview, or land you a job. And though you might receive all kinds of useful support, including a mass-mailing of your resume or inclusion into a database, it's unlikely anyone will actually pick up the phone and make a significant number of cold calls on your behalf. In the final analysis, the burden of marketing your availability will fall squarely upon your shoulders.

Keep these facts in mind when you consider the cost of using a retail outplacement firm. Depending on which services you're sold, you can spend anywhere from a few hundred to several thousand dollars. (It's not unheard of for unemployed candidates to pay as much as $10,000 for outplacement services.) "Watch out for any retail outfit that promises they'll find you a job," warns John Eichelberger, vice president of Drake Beam Morin, Inc., the largest corporate outplacement firm in the United States. "If what they promise sounds too good to be true, it probably is."

Testing the waters

One of the more common services offered by the hired guns falls under the category of "testing." Before you sign up, be sure you find out what the test results will tell you, and that the test you're given is reputable, and can be scored and interpreted accurately.

If you possess deeply hidden talents or have difficulty getting in touch with what really interests you, then test results may offer you a panacea of self-realization. And if you're changing careers, or you need the reassurance of a third party, a test may be just what the doctor ordered. Otherwise, be careful not to spend a lot of money needlessly documenting what you already know.

I took a career test several years ago when I lived in Los Angeles. At the time I was 33, and I'd just received my master's degree in music performance. My entire adult life had been spent as a professional musician, and I'd decided to make a career change. After a decade and a half of continual struggle (and an annual income that only once broke the five figure barrier), I'd had enough, and wanted out of the music business.

So I drove down to the University of Southern California career placement office, where, after paying a fee, I was subjected to a three-hour battery of personality, aptitude and intelligence tests.

Two weeks later, Robin, a counselor from the placement office, called to give me the results.

"Mr. Radin, we've scored the tests," she said.

"Great. What do they say?"

"Well, everything points in the same direction. In terms of your aptitudes and interests, we're pretty certain we know which career path you should follow."

"Really?" Maybe I'd make a terrific trial lawyer, or architect, or civil servant. "So what's the good news?"

Robin paused as if to build the suspense. She was well aware of the potential life-changing impact of her call. Finally she spoke.

"After carefully considering the results, Mr. Radin, it's apparent you'd be perfectly suited to a career as a professional musician."

Employment agencies: Pay as you go

Although the vast majority of headhunters have abandoned the practice of charging candidates fees for finding them jobs, this method (known in the placement business as "APF" or applicant-paid fee) remains a viable option for many people, especially those seeking entry-level or clerical positions.

Paid on a contingent basis, an employment agency will actively market your background to prospective companies. After you're placed, you'll owe the agency either a flat fee or a percentage of your first year's earnings. Agencies will usually help arrange financing for the fees, which range from around $1,200 to $3,000; and some will give discounts for cash payment.

Most headhunters cringe at the thought of charging fees to candidates, even though the APF method of personnel placement was prevalent until the early 1970s, when the EPF (employer-paid fee) system really took hold. In some states, EPF recruiters have led the fight to either curtail or abolish applicant-paid fees, since they feel the practice tarnishes their "management consultant" image.

Still, APF remains a big part of the employment picture in certain geographic markets. For example, more than 100 candidates paid to have themselves placed by Snelling Personnel Services, a well-known agency in Akron, Ohio, in 1990.

"Headhunters are just turning away good business," says Howard Rubin, Jr., vice president of Snelling. "I believe we should offer employment services to anyone who's willing to pay the fee. If a candidate needs the help we can provide, I'm certainly not going to say stand in his way."

If an applicant-paid employment agency isn't what you need, there are plenty of other third-party specialists willing to help.

> *Depending on your circumstances, the careful use of hired guns can give your job search a boost.*

9 The Power of Interview Preparation

Woody glanced nervously at the clock above his desk, trying unsuccessfully to conceal his anxiety. His job interview was scheduled for 2 p.m., and it was nearly noon already.

"Hey, it's OK," soothed Alice, Woody's co-worker. "A little novocaine, and you won't feel a thing. Who knows, if you don't squirm too much, maybe the dentist will give you a lollipop."

"Yeah, just what I need, with all my cavities." *Gosh, am I nervous,* thought Woody. *Why did I have to make such a big deal about going to the dentist?*

"Let's hope you won't have to go back for another visit."

Woody smiled. "Well, you never know." *Great. I'm sure everyone in the office can see right through my little white lie.*

"Anyway, good luck," Alice winked.

She knows! Oh, well, I can trust her. She's had a couple of toothaches herself, lately. I just hope I do all right at my interview this afternoon.

Which reminds me. I need to check my list to make sure I haven't forgotten anything. Let's see:

Seven keys to interview preparation

1. Resume, two copies.

2. Appropriate dress and appearance.

3. Directions to the company, parking instructions.

4. Name and title of the interviewer(s).

5. An understanding of the company's hiring procedure.

6. Background information on the interviewing company.

7. Complete list of questions I want to ask regarding:

   a. company
   b. industry
   c. position
   d. opportunity

OK, I guess I'm set. All I have to worry about now is giving a dynamite interview, and whether I fit the position they want to fill.

Win the battle in your tent

Woody was smart to prepare himself for his interview by making a list. That's because the interviewing process actually begins long before the first face-to-face meeting takes place.

Like Woody, you, too, can plot your course and remove any obstacles that might appear in advance, to improve your chances for success.

It's been said that Napoleon won his battles in his tent; that is, he did all the planning the night before the battle was joined, so that every contingency would be adequately covered. Interview preparation is similar. You never know exactly what will happen on the battlefield, but by being ready, you can eliminate a lot of the uncertainty, and know how to react to different scenarios.

Later, we'll look at ways to effectively conduct the interview itself; but for now, let's focus on the list, each item at a time.

1. The resume

Of course, bring a couple of copies, and be sure to *read* your resume before the interview, so you're completely familiar with everything you've written. Nothing is more embarrassing (or potentially fatal to your candidacy) than being quizzed on some aspect of your background that appears on the bottom of page 2—and not being able to remember the details.

You might also bring materials that would be particularly good at illustrating an important aspect of your work, such as creative designs, writing samples, and so forth. Just remember to use your better judgment.

I once interviewed an engineer who brought with him a lawn and garden string trimmer made by his current company, so he could show me the design improvements he'd made on the product. It turns out his engineering efforts had lowered the trimmer's cost to manufacture, which resulted in increased profits for his company. His version of "show-and-tell" was a bit extreme (my whole office was buzzing for weeks about my *Weed Eater* candidate), but at least his real-life picture told me a thousand words.

Be careful, though, not to overdo it with the props. College diplomas, letters of commendation, and company bowling trophies should be left at home. When in doubt, just bring your resume and your business card—they're the most important props you'll ever need.

It's a good idea to carry a leather folder or day runner with you so you can take notes or store written materials the company might hand you during the course of your interview. A briefcase is also fine, although I prefer a folder, which is lighter to carry, and less cumbersome. Always remember to bring a pen or pencil.

2. Appropriate dress and appearance

Much as I find some aspects of the *New Dress for Success* (Warner Books, 1988) formula as espoused by author and wardrobe consultant John T. Molloy a bit disheartening, there's simply no practical excuse for dressing any way other than the book suggests. Sure, we'd all like to think that we're being judged on our qualifications, skills, and depth of character. But the truth is, when it comes to interviewing, in most cases, clothes make the man or woman. To think any other way is to ignore reality.

Simply put, the more your appearance varies from the accepted norm, the less your chances become of getting the job. This means that if you're a male, you should wear a high-quality gray or navy blue wool or wool blend suit, a white shirt, a red tie, and black shoes, socks, and belt. If you're a female, you should also wear a suit or business dress, and scale way back on your makeup, jewelry and accessories. For both men and women, it's best to wear your hair in an unpretentious, understated style.

For nearly every professional candidate, the general rule surrounding attire is: The more conservative, the better. Of course, there are exceptions. If your industry is clothes conscious, (as in retail, hospitality or entertainment), then there may be certain fashion statements that might be considered acceptable or preferred. But for the vast majority of occupations, when in doubt, play it safe.

While it's true that you won't necessarily dress for work the way you'd dress for an interview, appearance is an important element in the interviewing protocol. You may not agree with the custom, but the choice is yours—you can either go with the flow, or take your chances.

The way you dress is particularly important if the job you're interviewing for requires you to make personal contact with those outside the company. Since your image or credibility with these people will be a big part of the job, then your prospective employer will put a great deal of emphasis on your appearance when it comes to evaluating your candidacy.

With some employers, appearance is a sort of sacred cow; and during the interviewing process, any deviation from the industry standard will lead to immediate rejection. Remember to ask yourself before you leave for an interview: Will my appearance play in Peoria? That is, will it be acceptable to the widest possible audience?

You might remember the giant oil company I told you about in the first chapter; and how their corporate obsession with appearance knocked out a perfectly qualified (but bearded) candidate.

It turns out I had another candidate scheduled to interview with the same company later in the week. This time, though, I wasn't going to make the mistake of sending him out without first checking to see what he looked like.

My plan was to pick him up at the airport and *hand deliver* him to the company. You can bet I wasn't about to have him show up wearing anything but the standard interviewing uniform. So the night before he flew into town, I called to give him explicit instructions on what to wear.

"Dave," I said, "I want to prepare you as well as I possibly can for your interview tomorrow. I'm going to get very specific about your appearance, because it's important to the company, and may very well affect their decision to hire you."

"OK, I can deal with that," said Dave.

"First of all, you're clean-shaven, aren't you?"

"Yes."

"Good. Do you have a clean, navy blue, pinstripe suit you can wear for your interview tomorrow?"

"Yes, I've got the suit."

"Fine. I want you to wear a white, cotton, button-down shirt. Do you have one?"

"Yes, I've got the shirt."

"Great. Now, do you have a dark red tie?"

"Yes, I've got the tie."

"Good. Can you wear black shoes, black socks, and a black belt?"

"No problem."

"All right. Do you need a haircut..."

"Wait a minute," Dave interrupted. "I think I know where this is all leading, and I want to assure you, everything's going to be fine."

"But I just want to make sure you fit in with the company's expectations..."

"I know, but I've been down this road before, and I know what kind of company I'll be dealing with."

"You mean...?"

"Don't worry," Dave said. "I vote Republican."

What I like about this story is that at the interview, the company fell in love with Dave, and hired him. I shudder to think what might have happened if he had dressed even a little bit differently (with brown shoes or a green tie, for example).

The reason I subscribe so thoroughly to the John T. Molloy *New Dress for Success* system is that first of all, it's totally objective. Through exhaustive research and experimentation, Molloy breaks down clothing and its psychological effect on people in a cold, scientific manner. And secondly, the system *works*.

Sure, it's boring, having to go to interviews dressed in a specific, premeditated uniform. But doing so takes all the guesswork out of what'll be successful and what won't. In a competitive job market, don't you want the odds on your side?

I once prepared an engineering candidate for an interview by asking him to wear a suit. The only one he had was several years old, and it was jet black. He kidded me about making him promise to wear his "undertaker's outfit" to a technical interview in the middle of the summer. But I stood my ground, feeling that the suit would improve his chance of getting hired.

A couple of days later, the interview took place in my office. True to his word, the candidate showed up, resplendent in his jet-black undertaker's suit. We had barely finished shaking hands when the employer strolled into my office, dressed in his work attire—a flannel shirt, jeans and sneakers!

After the interview was over, the candidate and I had a good belly laugh over the obvious discrepancy in apparel. Of course, we could afford to laugh, since the employer had just made the candidate a job offer.

3. Directions to the company, parking instructions

This might seem obvious, but again, there's a certain protocol to punctuality and manners when it comes to your grand entrance.

Try to get directions at least a day before your interview, so you don't get lost and arrive late. And here's a tip: Always bring some cash to pay for parking. Never ask an employer to validate your parking stub, or reimburse you for parking. Not only is it impolite, you'll create a negative impression, since it's considered common courtesy to pay your own expenses for a local interview.

If you're coming from out of town, then it's especially important to get directions. Naturally, if the expenses for your interviewing trip are going to be covered by the employer, wait until the interview has concluded (or better yet, the next day) to settle up. Usually, the company will prepay the air fare, or other major expenses, and will reimburse you for the rest, such as your car rental, cab fare, hotel room and meals. It's customary that you pick up certain non-essential expenses, such as long-distance phone calls from your hotel room, or the bar tab from the lounge in the hotel lobby.

A few years ago, a client company of mine flew a candidate to Los Angeles for an interview. The candidate, unfortunately, was unemployed at the time, and was in pretty dire financial straits. He charged the phone calls he made to his wife back in Wyoming and all his dry cleaning expenses (he only brought one shirt with him for two days of interviewing) to the company. When they got his expense voucher a few days later, they got pretty upset—they never expected to pay for all these add-ons. It was too bad, too, because he was generally well-received when he interviewed. I'd hate to think it was these little charges that convinced his prospective employer not to offer him the job.

The best time to arrive for an interview is precisely when you're scheduled, not early or late. It can irk an employer to be told that the candidate for a 2 p.m. appointment is waiting in the lobby at 1:35 p.m. The employer will either become distracted knowing there's someone hanging around waiting to see him, or he'll scramble to rearrange his schedule to accommodate the candidate, which disrupts the rest of his day. If your appointment is at 2, then arrive at 2.

If you're running late, call ahead to ask if you can reschedule for later the same day, or if not, later in the week. If something unexpected happens that you have no control over, simply explain the situation to the employer when you arrive.

I placed a candidate named Alan recently, who was over an hour late to his first interview. He'd been caught in a monstrous traffic jam and was unable to call ahead; but fortunately, he handled the situation like a pro. When he arrived, he apologized for being late, and got right down to the business of interviewing. He simply put all the anxiety and frustration behind him, so that he could concentrate on the reason he was there, not the reason he was late.

If you're ever caught in a situation like Alan was, stay cool, take a deep breath and remove whatever misfortune befell you from your mind.

4. The name and title of the interviewer(s)

The more information you arm yourself with going into an interview, the better. There are two reasons for this. First, you want to be adequately prepared for the interview itself. You might think of yourself as a pro football team, studying the films of next Sunday's opponent, in order to understand them better, and predict their moves.

Secondly, you want to avoid any surprises when you show up for the interview. It can take a lot of wind out of your sails if, for example, you get the impression you're going to meet the president of the company, and instead, your interview consists of 15 minutes in the personnel office, answering mundane questions about your college credits.

When you arrange the interview, find out who you'll be talking to, and what his or her function is within the company. Will you be speaking with the hiring manager? The manager from another department? The personnel director? The internal recruiter? A peer level employee or subordinate? A staff industrial psychologist?

You might already know the person. If that's the case, you're ahead of the game. If not, send out feelers among your own contacts within your industry, or look in your industry's trade publications to see if the person you're going to be meeting is distinguished in any way.

It's also helpful to find out whether you and the person you'll be meeting have any *commonalities* or interconnecting points of interest, in the way of origins ("Hey, you're also from Wisconsin?"), schools ("My brother went to Duke, too. How did you like it?"), professional achievements ("My article appeared in *Adweek* a month after yours did."), or personal interests ("I heard you were the Nebraska state pingpong champion. We'll have to get together sometime for a match."). These tidbits can break the ice when an interview begins, and create a bond with the interviewer.

To complete your understanding of the people you'll meet at the interview, you should probe for as much information as possible at the time the interview is being arranged. Let's say you'll be interviewing for a sales position, and that you'll be talking with Ms. Suzanne Whitaker. Be sure that you get the answers to the following questions:

- What's the correct spelling of Ms. Whitaker's name?
- What's her title?
- How long has she been with the company?
- Where did she work before?
- Is she the person I'd be reporting to?
- Who else will I be meeting?
- If there are others, what are their functions?
- How long shall I plan to spend interviewing?
- Will I need to arrive early to fill out an application, or complete any paperwork?

You can't know too much about the people you're going to meet, or too much about the sequence of events once the interviewing process has begun.

I arrived exactly on time once for an interview with the general manager of a company I wanted to work for. I assumed that he and I were going to begin our interview right away. Boy, was I wrong. After greeting me in the lobby, he led me to a little office, where I was given two hours of intelligence, aptitude and psychological tests. Had I not wanted the job so badly, I probably would have walked out in a huff. True, he never told me I'd have to take any tests; but then again, I never asked, either.

5. An understanding of the company's hiring procedure

How would you like to interview for a position you assumed the company wanted to fill immediately, only to find out that the target date for filling it was six months later? Or, how would you react if you were pressured to accept an offer following what you thought was only a "screening" interview? Or what would your opinion be of a company that made you wait six weeks until your second interview could be arranged? Most people find scenarios like these unnerving, to say the least.

While you can't change an employer's hiring procedure, you can at least prepare yourself mentally, and diffuse your own anxiety. By finding out what's in store following the interview, you can *desensitize* yourself to either the surprise attack or waiting game that's likely to come.

To correctly gauge the sequence of events surrounding or following your first interview, ask these questions:

- Can you describe to me, step by step, the hiring procedure for this position?

This is important to ask, because you want to find out if (and when) the company needs to schedule a second or third interview. Some companies will make hiring decisions on the spot; others will take months of meetings and endless signatures to process a simple request for a second interview.

- Will I be asked to take any tests?

And if so, what are they, and how long will they take to administer? Proctor & Gamble, for many of its professional positions, requires candidates to take a one-hour math and abstract reasoning test. Some companies require a full day of psychological, aptitude, technical skill and intelligence testing. With most companies, failure to pass the tests means automatic elimination from consideration.

Most drug tests are simply referred to as "physicals," and may take several days to schedule and process. Often, you'll have to use your own doctor or clinic.

- How long will it take before you reach a decision?

This will help you measure your progress through the hiring process, and could spare you from getting the jitters if you don't hear something immediately.

I once got bent out of shape because a new client company was taking a long time to make a decision whether to bring back one of my candidates for a second interview. Later, I found in my original notes that the company was right on schedule; they'd told me up front that it would take them several weeks to reach a decision. As it turns out, I had no reason to complain.

- Do you currently have any finalists?

This question lets you know if you've entered the race late, and your interview with the company is only a formality. In a situation like this, isn't it best to know where you stand?

- Who will be making the hiring decision?

Find out if the decision will be made by a committee. If it is, must the committee come to a *unanimous* agreement? Or, will the decision be based on the recommendation of a single person?

The more information you can dig up about the hiring procedure, the better you'll be able to give a more confident, thoughtful interview. What's more, arriving at an interview armed with a bastion of facts will help you shield yourself from the fear that occurs as a result of feeling out of control.

6. Background information on the company

Imagine for a moment that you're having dinner with a blind date. The waiter has just taken your orders, and your date turns to you and says, "I've heard a lot about you, and I'm especially intrigued by the years you spent in the Peace Corps. Tell me, did you find it exciting?"

If you're like most people, you'd be flattered by the fact that a complete stranger took enough interest in you to find out something about you before you met. And your opinion of the person doing the flattering would probably be bumped up a notch, too, knowing it took some initiative to do a little digging.

Employers are no different than the rest of us. They're proud of their companies and their accomplishments, and respond favorably to those who've taken the extra effort to get to know something about them in advance.

While the amount of background information you can gather about a company is practically endless, it would be ludicrous to try to become a walking encyclopedia of corporate trivia. However, knowing something in each of these categories should significantly improve your odds of getting hired:

- **The company's personnel.** Who the major players are, who was recently hired or let go. It's also a good idea to know something of the history of the company, and who the founders were. For example, if you were interviewing for IBM, it might be considered a *faux pas* to look puzzled and ask, "Who?" at mention of the name Thomas Watson, Sr.
- **The company's basic structure.** What products or services it provides to which customers, what the various divisions are, and whether it is privately or publicly held.
- **The company's vital signs.** How the company is doing financially. Is it solvent or struggling? Is it involved in a hostile takeover, or merging with another company? How's its stock faring? You get the idea. Many of my candidates like to look through *Value Line* before they interview, so they can talk intelligently about the company's financial picture.
- **The company's divisional or departmental details.** The changes that are taking place that could potentially affect the position you're interviewing for. Is there a new product introduction or marketing strategy in the works? Or how about an overhaul in the company's accounting methods, capital equipment or computer system?

By arriving for your interview adequately briefed, you'll make a strong impression on the interviewer. Best of all, you can spend your interviewing time discussing your background and the company's needs, not the corporate biography, or company financial report.

7. Complete list of questions you want to ask

What happens when you go to the grocery store without a list? If you're like me, you'll be halfway home before you remember the item or items you failed to buy.

The questions you ask during an interview will not only satisfy your own needs, they'll indicate to the interviewer the things that are important to you, and reveal the way you process information and formulate opinions.

During the course of an interview, your dialogue with the other person will spawn a number of questions spontaneously. However, there may be important issues to discuss that will never come up unless you take the initiative. For that reason, you should bring a list of questions with you that will address these issues, so that you don't leave the interview uninformed.

Premeditated questions can be grouped into four different categories:

- **Company** questions deal with the organization, direction, policies, stability, growth, market share and new products or services of the prospective company or department.
- **Industry** questions deal with the health, growth, change, technological advancement and personnel of the industry as a whole.
- **Position** questions deal with the scope, responsibilities, travel, compensation policies and reporting structure of the position you're interviewing for.
- **Opportunity** questions deal with your own potential for growth or advancement within the company or its divisions, and the likely timetable for promotion.

You may have specific interests or concerns surrounding topics in each category. For example, if you're interviewing with a computer manufacturer, you may want to ask about the future growth of the industry. Or, let's say you're interviewing for a position with a company that's known for its high rate of personnel turnover. You might want to prepare a carefully worded question that deals with that issue.

But leave your laundry list

Naturally, you need to be careful not to come on too strong by asking too many questions—it may turn the interviewer off.

141

Presumably, if there's mutual interest, you'll get all your questions answered at a subsequent interview. The general rule of thumb is to limit the number of premeditated questions to about a dozen or less. While it's true that you'll be interviewing the company as much as they'll be interviewing you, the last thing you want to do is turn a dialogue into an inquisition, or come across as a walking encyclopedia of corporate trivia.

You should also be aware that there's one specific taboo to first-level interviewing, in terms of the questions you should ask. *Never, ever bring up the issue of salary or benefits.* If the employer initiates a dialogue surrounding these issues, and asks if you have any questions, fine.

But if it appears to the employer that your primary motivation for changing jobs is the new company's compensation or benefit package, you'll be out the door quicker than a bolt of lightning. Employers get chills of fear and loathing when they think you're only on the job market to feather your nest at their expense. They visualize your employment with them as a short-term, non-committal, career-leveraging maneuver, and understandably, want to avoid being victimized.

Early in my career as a recruiter, I arranged an interview for a qualified candidate with a client company. After the interview, I called Shelly, the employer, to debrief her.

"Well, your candidate didn't do so well," Shelly said.

"Really? I thought he had the perfect background."

"That wasn't the problem. I just didn't like the way he handled the interview."

"What happened?"

"I spent over an hour with him, telling him everything about the company, and introducing him to all the key people," Shelly said. "I even gave him an extensive tour of the manufacturing area."

"And then?"

"And then, I brought him back to my office, and we sat down to talk about what he'd seen. I asked him if he had any questions."

"And did he?"

"Yes. That's when the interview ended. He looked me straight in the eye and asked, 'What are your benefits?'"

"And?"

"And I got up," Shelly said, "and walked him right out the door."

Don't misunderstand me. The candidate's actions in no way reflected on his abilities or his character; his intentions were perfectly honorable. But after that incident (which cost the candidate a job and me a placement fee), I learned to caution interviewees not to initiate the subject of salary or benefits.

My suggestion is to take the *John F. Kennedy* approach to interviewing: "Ask not what your company can do for you, ask what you can do for your company."

This way, you can present yourself as a loyal, hard-working, virtuous and dedicated candidate, rather than as an opportunistic job-hopper who'd prefer to live off the fat of the land.

While it's unthinkable to accept or even consider a job without first knowing the financial rewards (or the details of the benefit package), there are better and more timely ways to broach the subject, without endangering your candidacy.

Interview preparation is perhaps the single most overlooked aspect of the job changing process. A candidate who's fired up and ready to go at the time of the interview has a tremendous advantage over a candidate who's not.

> *The more carefully you prepare for your interview, the better your chances of getting hired.*

10 How to Master the Art of Interviewing

Some people have the notion that in order to get a job offer, it's necessary to dazzle the interviewer with all sorts of slick, well-rehearsed answers to interview questions, as if an employment interview is a battle of wits, or war of nerves.

I meet with candidates like this all the time in my office. They usually come across as well-heeled yuppies with MBAs tucked under one arm and *The Wall Street Journal* under the other. I patiently listen to a lot of fashionable business school babble about "proactive feedback forecasting" and "heuristic negative-balance task prioritizing"—and wonder what the heck they're talking about!

They've got pat answers for every conceivable question, and tell me everything they think I want to hear. The only problem is, I've heard it all before.

Don't get me wrong. These types of candidates have been thoroughly coached in the competitive style of interviewing, and are sophisticated in the way they handle themselves. But I also feel badly for them, knowing how exhausting it must be trying to operate from behind a facade.

Relax—let down your guard

The truth is, giving an electrifying performance isn't all that necessary to getting the job you want—the interview is only one of four factors affecting any hiring decision. The others are: past experience (the "resume"), test results, and references. That means that you can give a straightforward, functional interview and still be hired, based on the strength of one or more of the other factors.

Besides, a critical dimension of every hiring decision is out of your control anyway: the element of *personal chemistry,* or shared values. There's simply no way to rehearse for whether two people will like each other. And if you fake the way you feel about someone else, you'll risk being exposed for fraud; or end up unhappy at the job, either of which will have defeated the whole purpose of interviewing for a new job in the first place.

There's no need to alter your identity for the sake of an interview. The best thing you can do is to relax, and use the client-centered method of interviewing—a method that allows you to effectively interview, without changing your personality.

The client-centered method

A few years ago, I was introduced to a book written by Dr. Carl Rogers (1902-1987), an influential clinical psychologist. Entitled **Client-Centered Therapy**, the book told of Rogers' method of counseling, in which he related to his patients (or "clients") with an aura of unconditional acceptance. During the sessions, Dr. Rogers didn't necessarily agree or disagree with what his clients told him; all he did was acknowledge that he understood what they said, through a variety of techniques, such as paraphrasing and active listening.

These techniques enabled Dr. Rogers to establish *empathy* with his clients, so they'd feel comfortable, and non-threatened. Once empathy was established, Dr. Rogers could communicate freely and provide the therapy his clients needed, without the barriers that normally inhibit a discussion between two "unequal" parties.

It turns out that empathy can also be a very powerful tool for settings other than counseling. In fact, empathy can used effectively any time you want to exchange ideas with another person.

When you think about it, that's exactly what an interview is: an exchange of ideas with another person. And empathy is your most powerful tool.

Here's how it applies

Webster defines empathy as the "intellectual or emotional identification with another person's thoughts, feelings or attitudes." So that begs the question: What are the thoughts, feelings or attitudes of someone who's conducting an interview?

The answer is: *You don't know.*

If you make assumptions, you've missed the whole point of client-centered interviewing. Only by listening carefully and asking questions will you find out the real needs of the interviewer. What's the point of "selling yourself" to someone unless you know what they're buying?

Let's say you're a 6-foot-7-inch chess master and your last name is Schwartz-Hernandez. You graduated from Harvey Mudd College with a major in animal husbandry. You've spent the last five years selling insurance, and you just finished interviewing for a technical writing position with a company that makes concrete geese.

And they offered you the job.

Now, was it because your last name is Schwartz-Hernandez? Or because you went to Harvey Mudd College? Or because you used to sell insurance?

None of the above! It was because the interviewer *liked* you, and thought you could do the job. He liked you because of the way you took time to understand his needs, and probe for the qualities he was looking for in an employee. During the interview, you made discoveries that allowed you to build a strong case for why the company ought to hire you. And, oh yes. It didn't seem to hurt that the interviewer, like you, plays a mean game of chess and studied animal husbandry in college.

By contrast, I recently arranged an interview between a high-level candidate from a big company and the president of a small company.

After the interview, the candidate told me he had no idea what the company's needs were; that the president never revealed to him anything about the company's growth plans, new products or financial outlook. Later, when I called the president to debrief him, I found out why.

"Your candidate never shut up," said the president. "He was so intent on telling me how great he was, and what an impact he could make on my company, he never gave me the chance to talk."

"So what did you do?" I asked.

"I finally gave up trying. In the three hours he was here, he never bothered to ask anything about me or my company."

Fundamentals of a successful interview

To a large degree, the success of your interview will depend on your ability to discover needs and empathize with the interviewer. You can do this by asking questions that verify your understanding of what the interviewer has just said, without editorializing or expressing an opinion. By establishing empathy in this manner, you'll be in a better position to freely exchange ideas and demonstrate your suitability for the job.

In addition to empathy, there are four other *intangible* fundamentals to a successful interview. These intangibles will influence the way your personality is perceived, and will affect the degree of rapport or personal chemistry you'll share with the employer.

1. **Enthusiasm**. Leave no doubt as to your level of interest in the job. You may think it's unnecessary to do this, but employers often choose the more enthusiastic candidate in the case of a two-way tie. Besides, it's best to keep your options open—wouldn't you rather be in a position to turn down an offer, than have a prospective job evaporate from your grasp by giving a lethargic interview?

2. **Technical interest**. Employers look for people who love what they do, and get excited by the prospect of getting into the nitty-gritty of the job.

3. **Confidence**. No one likes a braggart, but the candidate who's sure of his or her abilities will almost certainly be more favorably received.

4. **Intensity**. The last thing you want to do is come across as "flat" in your interview. There's nothing inherently wrong with being a laid-back person; but sleepwalkers rarely get hired.

By the way, most employers are aware of how stressful it can be to interview for a new position, and will do everything they can to put you at ease.

The other fundamentals

Since interviewing also involves the exchange of *tangible* information, make sure to:

1. **Present your background** in a thorough and accurate manner.
2. **Gather data** concerning the company, the industry, the position and the specific opportunity.
3. **Link your abilities** with the company needs in the mind of the employer.
4. **Build a strong case** for why the company should hire you, based on the discoveries you make from building rapport and asking the right questions.

Both for your sake and the employer's, never leave an interview without exchanging fundamental information. The more you know about each other, the more potential you'll have for establishing rapport, and making informed decisions.

Interviewing strategy

There's a definite *protocol* to interviewing, consisting of a specific set of do's and don'ts, along with a few common-sense techniques you can use to increase your odds of getting the job.

Let me share with you a few of the strategies I've learned from the hundreds of interviews I've arranged, some of which were successful, and some of which were unmitigated disasters. The first strategy deals with the most common (and costly) mistake that candidates make: the tendency to talk too much.

The short and long of it

There are two ways to answer interview questions: the *short version* and the *long version*. When a question is open-ended, I always suggest to candidates that they say, "Let me give you the short version. If we need to explore some aspect of the answer more fully, I'd be happy to go into greater depth, and give you the long version."

The reason you should respond this way is because it's often difficult to know what type of answer each question will need. A question like, "What was your most difficult assignment?" might take anywhere from 30 seconds to 30 minutes to answer, depending on the detail you choose to give.

Therefore, you must always remember that the interviewer is the one who asked the question. So you should tailor your answer to what he or she needs to know, without a lot of extraneous rambling or superfluous explanation. Why waste time and create a negative impression by giving a sermon when a short prayer would do just fine?

Let's suppose you were interviewing for a sales management position, and the interviewer asked you, "What sort of sales experience have you had in the past?"

Well, that's exactly the sort of question that can get you into trouble if you don't use the short-version/long-version method. Most people would just start rattling off everything in their memory that relates to their sales experience. Though the information might be useful to the interviewer, your answer could get pretty complicated unless it's neatly packaged.

One way to answer the question might be, "I've held sales positions with three different consumer product companies over a nine-year period. Where would you like me to start?"

Or, you might simply say, "Let me give you the short version first, and you can tell me where you want to go into more depth. I've had nine years experience in consumer product sales with three different companies, and held the titles of district, regional and national sales manager. What aspect of my background would you like to concentrate on?"

By using this method, you telegraph to the interviewer that your thoughts are well-organized, and that you want to understand the intent of the question before you travel too far in a direction neither of you wants to go. After you get the green light, you can spend your interviewing time discussing in detail the things that are important, not whatever happens to pop into your mind.

Don't talk yourself out of a job

I've got a friend who's the hiring manager of a soup company. He told me once that he brought a candidate into his office to make him a job offer. An hour later, the candidate left. I asked my friend if he had hired the candidate.

"No," he said. "I tried. But the candidate wouldn't stop talking long enough for me to make him an offer."

Don't misinterpret me. I'm not suggesting that an interview should consist of a series of monosyllabic grunts. It's just that nothing turns off an employer faster than a windbag candidate.

By using the short-version/long-version method to answer key questions, you'll never talk yourself out of a job.

The prudent use of questions

Beware: An interview will quickly disintegrate into an interrogation or monologue unless you ask some high-quality questions of your own. Candidate questions are the lifeblood of any successful interview, because they:

- **Create dialogue**, which will not only enable the two of you to learn more about each other, but will help you visualize what it'll be like working together once you've been hired.
- **Clarify your understanding** of the company and the position responsibilities.
- **Indicate your grasp** of the fundamental issues discussed so far.
- **Reveal your ability** *to probe* beyond the superficial.
- **Challenge the employer** to reveal his or her own depth of knowledge, or commitment to the job.

Your questions should always be slanted in such a way as to show empathy, interest or understanding of the employer's needs. After all, the reason you're interviewing is because the employer's company has some piece of work that needs to be completed, or a problem that needs correcting. Here are some questions that have proven to be very effective:

- What's the most important issue facing your department?
- How can I help you accomplish this objective?
- How long has it been since you first identified this need?
- How long have you been trying to correct it?
- Have you tried using your present staff to get the job done? What was the result?
- What other means have you used? For example, have you brought in independent contractors or temporary help? Or have you recently hired people who haven't worked out?
- Is there any particular skill or attitude you feel is critical to getting the job done?
- Is there a unique aspect of my background that you'd like to exploit in order to help accomplish your objectives?

Questions like these will not only give you a sense of the company's goals and priorities, they'll indicate to the interviewer your concern for satisfying the company's objectives.

Evidence of corporate culture

One of the main objectives when interviewing is to determine whether you and the prospective employer are well-matched in terms of values. If you're comfortable with the physical environment and the feeling you get from those you interview, then you're "in tune" with the corporate culture. If, on the other hand, your gut feeling tells you that something is out of whack, then you should definitely exercise caution before you accept the company's offer.

Be on the lookout for physical evidence of corporate culture such as:

- **Bulletin boards**. What sort of notices are posted? Are they friendly and positive or angry and negative in tone? For example, do you see announcements for company events such as picnics, softball games and work-related seminars? Or for petition signings, protest rallies and strikes?

- **Honor rolls and award plaques.** Does the company visibly demonstrate its appreciation for loyal and/or outstanding service?
- **Internal communications.** Does the company publish a newsletter, produce a video or host a quarterly or annual meeting for its employees? If so, are the communications upbeat and informative?
- **Cleanliness.** Is the place kept neat, or is it a repository of dust and junk accumulated by company *schlumpers*?
- **Ventilation and/or air quality.** Is the place too warm, too cool or too stuffy? Do the employees smoke cigarettes? If so, are nonsmokers provided with protected areas or electrostatic air cleaners?
- **Adequate lighting.** Can the employees see well enough to do their jobs? Or does a dark, cavernous environment seem more suitable for a mutant strain of office bats?
- **Business machines.** Are the copiers, computers, typewriters, telephones and fax machines functional and reasonably up-to-date?
- **Manufacturing capability.** Is the production area equipped with machines that are in working order and of competitive quality? Is the shop floor well-organized, or more like Uncle Murray's garage?
- **Kitchen/lunchroom area.** Is there a clean, quiet communal space set aside for having lunch or taking a coffee break?
- **Pictures, posters and artwork.** Does the company take pride in its physical appearance by investing in attractive artwork or photographs? Or are the walls cluttered with rummage sale remnants?

You can learn a lot about an organization from your first impressions. For example, I took an office tour of a prospective client company not long ago. Tacked on the wall in plain view of the engineering department (and visible to anyone who happened to walk by) was a large, full-color beer company advertising poster, featuring a scantily-clad female model in a suggestive pose. I was embarrassed by what I saw; and in fact, the poster's presence figured into my decision not to take the employer on as a client. I couldn't in good faith recommend to my candidates a company whose corporate culture fostered what I considered to be an insensitive, insulting attitude toward women.

Whistle while you work

Corporate culture is most commonly defined as the collective attitude, ethical standards, personality and intensity level of the employees. Observe the people at the company as you interview. Are they bustling about with smiles on their faces, or are they grumpy, sleepy or dopey?

A sure-fire tip-off to the social psychology of the organization will come directly from the interviewer himself. Examine carefully the messages imbedded in his body language, appearance, speech patterns and immediate surroundings.

For example, where does he ask you to sit when the interview begins? Across from his desk? With him at a round conference table? Or in one of two chairs set a right angles? What's the physical appearance of the interviewer? Well-groomed or rumpled? Down-to-earth or pretentious?

Is the interviewer's office nicely put together and well-organized? Or is it messy and out of control? What sorts of paraphernalia adorn the interviewer's desk? Photos of his family? Bowling trophies? Board of health citations?

Does the interviewer put you at ease, or try to intimidate you? Is he overly formal? Does he ask you to refer to him by his first name or by his title? Do you feel comfortable with his facial expressions? How about his physical presence? Does he establish and maintain eye contact? Does he tend to crowd you? Does he use coarse language, or exhibit racial, religious or gender prejudices? Does he tell off-color jokes? Does he seem to treat his co-workers and subordinates with dignity? Or with disdain?

Look for other signs that might reflect the corporate culture. During the interview, does the employer focus his complete attention on your conversation, or does he become easily distracted? Is he forthright about the company's financial health and future outlook? Does he encourage you to talk with other employees? Or is he afraid of what they might say?

In the final analysis, the most accurate indicator of corporate culture is going to be the company's president or CEO. After all, an organization is only the length and shadow of its leader. Try to find out what the head honcho is like, and if at all possible, arrange a brief interview. Chances are, if you hit it off with the person at the top, you'll probably fit into the culture. Otherwise, you'll really be taking a risk.

Before you decide to settle into a new position, ask yourself whether the prospective company is a place you would comfortably call "home" for eight hours a day.

Don't be sold a bill of goods

At some point during the interview, the employer will probably make an effort to "sell" you on the opportunity of working for his or her company. This is the time to really fine-tune your listening, since the interviewer now has a chance to express a wide variety of feelings about the organization. See if you can measure the interviewer's degree of enthusiasm, and look for any obvious (or subliminal) signs of doubt, reservation or dread. If you need more information (or you're not completely sold), you might ask these five questions:

1. After this project is finished, what's next on your agenda? How would I fit in?

2. If I'm hired, I intend to help the company the best I can over the course of several years. Can you tell me what sort of (leadership/management/technical) opportunities will exist within your organization for someone like me?

3. I don't mean to sound blunt, but tell me something: Why should I quit my present job to come to work here?

4. What is it that first attracted you to this company?

5. Does the position I'm interviewing for have a history of turnover? (To be asked if you're being considered as a replacement for someone who's left the company.)

If you're not clear about something the interviewer tells you, by all means speak up. Your interest in gathering accurate information won't annoy the interviewer; it'll only enhance your ability to carefully analyze the attractiveness of the position, and your compatibility with the company.

Listen very closely to what the interviewer has to say. It would be a real tragedy to accept a job, only to find out later that you misunderstood the nature of the job, or were sold a bill of goods.

Give it some thought

Here are seven of the most commonly asked interviewing questions. Do yourself—and the prospective employer—a favor, and give them some thought before the interview occurs.

1. Why do you want this job?
2. Why do you want to leave your present company?
3. Where do you see yourself in five years?
4. What are your personal goals and interests?
5. What are your strengths? Weaknesses?
6. What do you like most about your current company?
7. What do you like least about your current company?

The last question is probably the hardest to answer: *What do you like least about your present company?*

I've found that rather than pointing out the faults of other people ("I can't stand the office politics," or, "I don't get along with my boss"), it's best to place the burden on yourself ("I feel I'm ready to exercise a new set of professional muscles," or, "The type of technology I'm interested in isn't available to me now.").

By answering in this manner, you'll avoid pointing the finger at someone else, or coming across as a whiner or complainer. It does no good to speak negatively about others.

I suggest you think through the answers to the above questions for two reasons.

First, it won't help your chances any to hem and haw over fundamental issues such as these. (The answers you give to these types of questions should be *no-brainers*.)

And secondly, the questions will help you evaluate your career choices before spending time and energy on an interview. If you don't feel comfortable with the answers you come up with, maybe the new job isn't right for you.

Money, money, money

There's a good chance you'll be asked about your current and expected level of compensation. Here's the way to handle the following questions:

1. *What are you currently earning?*

   Answer: "My compensation, including bonus, is in the high 40s. I'm expecting my annual review next month, and that should put me in the low 50s."

2. *What sort of money would you need in order to come to work for our company?*

   Answer: "I feel that the *opportunity* is the most important issue, not salary. If we decide to work with each other, I'm sure you'll make me a fair offer."

Notice the way a *range* was given as the answer to the first question, not a specific dollar figure. However, if the interviewer presses for an exact answer, then by all means, be precise, in terms of salary, bonus, benefits, expected increase and so forth.

In answer to the second question, if the interviewer tries to zero in on your expected compensation, you should also suggest a range, as in, "I would need something in the low to mid 50s." Getting locked in to an exact figure may work against you later, in one of two ways: Either the number you give is lower than you really want to accept; or the number appears too high or too low to the employer, and an offer never comes. By using a range, you're more likely to keep your options open.

Some questions you can count on

There are four types of questions that interviewers like to ask.

1. There are the *resume* questions. These relate to your past experience, skills, job responsibilities, education, upbringing, personal interests and so forth.

   Resume questions require accurate, objective answers, since your resume consists of facts that tend to be quantifiable (and verifiable). Try to avoid answers that exaggerate your achievements, or appear to be opinionated, vague or egocentric.

2. Interviewers will usually want you to comment on your abilities, or assess your past performance. They will ask *self-appraisal* questions like, "What do you think is your greatest asset?" or, "Can you tell me something you've done that was very creative?"

3. Interviewers like to know how you respond to different stimuli. *Situation* questions ask you to explain certain actions you took in the past, or require that you explore hypothetical scenarios that may occur in the future. "How would you stay profitable during a recession?" or, "How would you go about laying off 1,300 employees?" or, "How would you handle customer complaints if the company drastically raised its prices?" are typical situation questions.

4. Some employers like to test your mettle with *stress* questions such as, "After you die, what would you like your epitaph to read?" or, "If you were to compare yourself to any U.S. president, who would it be?" or, "It's obvious your background makes you

totally unqualified for this position. Why should we even waste our time talking?"

Stress questions are designed to evaluate your emotional reflexes, creativity or attitudes while you're under pressure. Since off-the-wall or confrontational questions tend to jolt your equilibrium, or put you in a defensive posture, the best way to handle them is to stay calm and give carefully considered answers.

Whenever I hear a stress question, I immediately think of the Miss Universe beauty pageant. The finalists are asked before a live television audience of 3.5 billion people to give heartfelt and earnest responses to incongruous questions like, "What would you tell the leaders of all the countries on earth to do to promote world peace?"

Of course, your sense of humor will come in handy during the entire interviewing process, just so long as you don't go over the edge. I heard of a candidate once who, when asked to describe his ideal job, replied, "To have beautiful women rub my back with hot oil." Needless to say, he wasn't hired.

Even if it were possible to anticipate every interview question, memorizing dozens of stock answers would be impractical, to say the least. The best policy is to review your background, your priorities and your reasons for considering a new position; and to handle the interview as honestly as you can. If you don't know the answer to a question, just say so, or ask for a moment to think about your response.

Having the "magic answer" at the tip of your tongue can actually work against you. One of my client companies declined to offer a candidate a job because he came up with a correct, prepackaged answer for every question they asked him. "Slick Nick" became the company's not-too-flattering nickname for an otherwise qualified candidate.

Wrapping it up

At the conclusion of your interview, you can wrap up any unfinished business you failed to cover so far, and begin to explore the future of your candidacy. To do so, you'll need some information, which the following questions should help you gather:

1. Have we covered everything we need to?
2. What's the next step?
3. When do you plan on making a hiring decision?
4. Assuming you have an interest in me, who will be contacting me, and when?
5. When do you want to schedule my physical exam, or any of the tests you give to candidates?
6. Is there anything you'd like me to provide you, such as a list of references or a sample of my work?

If the employer says that everything has gone well, and the company would like to schedule another interview, see if you can nail down the time and date before you leave. If they need to "think it over," ask when you can call to set up another appointment.

During your interview wrap-up, it's a good practice to make the interviewer aware of other opportunities you're exploring, as long as they're genuine, and their timing has some bearing on your own decision-making.

For example, if you're currently under consideration with another company, be sure to tell the interviewer. You might say something like, "I interviewed with Acme Tool last week, and they've asked me back for a second meeting tomorrow," or, "I think it's only fair to tell you that I have an offer pending from Beaver Tree Service, and they're expecting a decision by the first of next week." Use your best judgment when sharing this information. If it jeopardizes your confidentiality with another prospective company, then keep its name out of it.

The fact that you're actively exploring other opportunities may affect the speed with which the company makes its hiring decision. It may even positively influence the eventual outcome, since the company may want to act quickly so as not to lose you.

However, your other activity should be presented in the spirit of assistance to the interviewer, not as a thinly veiled threat or negotiating tactic. No one likes to feel manipulated or pressured, and if the interviewer senses that he's being hustled or backed into a corner, you may find yourself the victim of your own wheeling and dealing.

I'd advise you to play it straight with the interviewer. Otherwise, you may risk your candidacy over a silly game of "employment chicken."

Play your cards now

If there are any potential problems or possible delays that might affect your "hire-ability," such as contractual obligations, personal commitments, visa or clearance considerations, or pre-scheduled vacations, you should bring them up at this point, as a courtesy to the employer.

The interviewer will appreciate your candor, since this information will be helpful to the company when a decision is made. By putting all your cards on the table at the beginning, you'll prevent the employer from feeling "sandbagged" later.

By volunteering pertinent information, you'll also give the company a feel for when you can start work, and provide them with a head start if they need to take any action on your behalf.

For example, you may need legal assistance in changing your right-to-work status if you've got a green card or student visa. Or, if the job requires a security clearance, physical examination or college transcripts, you can save time by getting things rolling right away.

Breaking up is hard to do

There are going to be times when you simply aren't interested in the new company or the position. In such a case, it's best to let the interviewer know, rather than waste each other's time.

Conversely, there'll be times when it's fairly obvious that the company doesn't like you, or you aren't the right person for the job. Again, I've found that it's better to make the break early on, rather than expend needless emotional energy later.

Here are some ways to communicate your feelings, or test for their disinterest:

- I get the feeling this isn't the right job for me. What's your opinion?
- I've got an offer pending from another company, which I think I'd be better suited for. Why don't we just shake hands and call it a day?
- I know someone who'd be much better for this job than I would. Can I give you her name?
- I'm afraid the job you're trying to fill is a mismatch for my skills and interests. However, I'd appreciate it if you'd keep my name on file, in case a different position comes up.

Depending on the interviewer's response, you'll know where you stand. Acceptance of your offer to terminate the interview will confirm your suspicions. On the other hand, if the employer resists your attempts to break away, you may need to consider the position in a new light.

Reading the buy signals

Selling professionals look for *buy signals* to help them gauge the prospect's level of interest, or predict the outcome of a presentation. They've learned that buy signals are like little *clues* that the other person telegraphs subconsciously when the buying hormones start flowing.

An interview is similar to a sales presentation. It follows, then, that the more buy signals you receive, the greater your chances are of closing the sale, or being hired.

Buy signals usually appear as questions. By recognizing certain questions as obvious buy signals, you can control your interview by honing in on them. The frequency and timing of the buy signals you receive will give you a feel for how the interview is going, and what to expect later. Generally, you can measure the probability of getting an offer based on the number of buy signals you were given, and the quality of your answers.

Here are some interview questions that can usually be interpreted as buy signals:

- Would you feel comfortable working here?
- Is there anything you don't understand about the position?
- Do you see any obvious differences in the way you and I think?
- Would you be interested in taking a tour of our facility?
- Have you discussed this job with your family? If so, how do they feel about it?
- Where else are you interviewing?
- Do you have any other offers pending?
- How soon could you start?
- Would you like to discuss our benefit package?
- What sort of salary would you be interested in?
- What would it take to get you on board?

Another obvious sign of an interviewer's interest is an extended interview; that is, one that lasts more than an hour or two. Buy signals might also include: being invited to lunch; being introduced to other interviewers or company officials; or being asked to return for another interview.

Although there's no guarantee that a lot of pointed questions from the interviewer will result in a job offer, you can't fail to improve your odds by recognizing buy signals.

The thank-you letter

The purpose of a thank-you letter is to show your sincere appreciation to the interviewer for spending time with you, and to keep your name "in his face."

In today's market, a thank-you letter is considered a professional courtesy. In a best-case scenario, a strong letter will reinforce any bond you and the interviewer may have formed. However, if the company has no interest in you, it's doubtful that a thank-you letter will do much to turn things around. In

A Standard Thank-You Letter

April 1, 1993

Mr. Andrew Sinaiko, Publisher
VIRGINIA BUSINESS
411 East Franklin St., Suite 105
Richmond, VA 23219

Dear Mr. Sinaiko:

Thank you for spending time with me last Tuesday. I feel our meeting was productive, and that I was able to gain a clear understanding of the needs of your department, and the responsibilities of the managing editor position you wish to fill.

The opportunity with VIRGINA BUSINESS appears to be very exciting, and I am certain my background would represent a positive addition to your staff.

If you have any further questions, please do not hesitate to call.

Sincerely,

John D. Holmes

John D. Holmes

cc: Goodloe Suttler, VP Human Resources

fact, a poorly conceived letter could even damage the positive impression you might have created during your recent interview.

Here are five pitfalls to avoid:

1. **You fail to proofread your letter.** Unfortunately, you make a spelling error or typo, which does nothing to improve the company's impression of you.

2. **You unwittingly call attention to an area of concern.** For example, you write, "I feel strongly that my customer service background will be a tremendous asset to the company." For all you know, the company liked everything about you *except* your customer service background. As the old saying goes, "Let a sleeping dog lie."

3. **You unnecessarily apologize for the way you interviewed.** "Sorry I made such a fool of myself yesterday," you write. "I'm ordinarily pretty good with numbers."

4. **You shamelessly beg for the job.** "If you just give me a chance, I promise you'll never regret it."

5. **You brag about your abilities, or criticize the competition.** "It should be obvious from our meeting that I'm clearly more qualified than the other candidates."

If you write a thank-you letter, take care in its design and construction. Use a high-quality typewriter or word processor, and by all means, make the letter as brief and antiseptic as possible.

The second-level interview

Most companies require at least two interviews before a decision can be made, or an offer can be extended.

You should treat your second-level interview much like your first, in that you want to be adequately prepared by the time you arrive. Presumably, your list of questions will have become pretty well focused, since you've had adequate time to ponder what was said at the first interview.

Make sure to get these questions answered, because the second meeting will probably be your last opportunity to collect information about the job. (Third- and fourth-level interviews are relatively rare.)

Your second-level interview will give you and the employer the chance to learn more about each other, and to delve more deeply into the details surrounding the position, the company, the industry and your potential career opportunities within the organization.

In addition, you'll now be able to zero in on your salary requirements, benefits and relocation package; topics that were probably glossed over in your initial interview.

Second-level interviews are generally reserved for those candidates who are considered to be the finalists for a specific position. However, as a finalist, it doesn't necessarily mean that you should expect to receive an offer during your meeting if all goes well. Companies usually like to take time to assess the information they've gathered.

As a result, the decision-making process could take anywhere from a couple of days to several weeks to resolve, depending on the urgency of filling the position, the number of decision-makers involved, the number of finalists yet to be interviewed, and countless other variables.

If you're working through a recruiter (or you're in a position to make a tactful inquiry on your own), find out if your second-level interview will be an *offer interview*. If it is, you can begin to make the necessary preparations to put the deal together and set a start date.

Following up

If you haven't heard anything immediately following your interview or thank-you letter, you might want to place a call to the interviewer, to find out where you stand. Or, if you're working through a headhunter, you'll want to stay in touch so that he or she can monitor your status. (Companies rarely send letters of regret, so if the news is bad, you'll have to dig it up on your own.)

Be sure to keep the interviewer informed of any changes on your end that may affect the company's decision, such as an offer from another organization, or an out-of-town trip that will take you out of circulation.

And remember to maintain a positive attitude. In today's job market, you'd be surprised how often victory is snatched from the jaws of defeat. If, after several weeks you haven't heard anything, and you're truly interested in working for the company, give them a call directly. You'll get either a sense of closure, or a reason to keep your hopes alive.

Your interviewing skill, preparation and follow-up will affect your chances of getting the job.

11 Putting the Deal Together

Let's assume the interview went well, and there's sincere and mutual interest on both sides.

Now you need to decide two things: first, whether the new position is right for you; and if so, what sort of offer you'd be willing to accept.

To evaluate the pros and cons, think back to the material we covered in the first chapter. Does the new job meet the criteria you spelled out, and improve your level of personal and professional satisfaction? Or will it simply offer you a rehash of what you already have? Hopefully, the unique qualities you're seeking will be within your grasp.

Keeping score

If you're not sure about the new job, or need help in being more objective, take the following test as a way to compare the two positions. You should be able to get a feel for how the job you interviewed for stacks up against your current position by selecting which considerations best suit your needs.

The position comparison test can be "scored" two different ways. You can either tally the totals (the best job has the highest score); or you can use the test as a way to examine your priorities.

Let's suppose your score was 15 to 7, in favor of the new company. Does that mean you should change jobs?

169

Position Comparison

Check your preferences.

Old Job	New Job	Consideration
❑	❑	Position title
❑	❑	Supervisory responsibility
❑	❑	Project authority
❑	❑	Decision-making autonomy
❑	❑	Freedom to implement ideas
❑	❑	Freedom to effect change
❑	❑	Promotion potential
❑	❑	Challenge of tasks
❑	❑	Appropriateness of expectations
❑	❑	Access to skill training
❑	❑	Professional growth potential
❑	❑	Company/industry growth
❑	❑	Company/industry stability
❑	❑	Starting salary
❑	❑	Future compensation
❑	❑	Company benefits/perks
❑	❑	Commuting distance
❑	❑	Travel requirements
❑	❑	Working environment
❑	❑	Rapport with co-workers
❑	❑	Rapport with management
❑	❑	Comfort with corporate culture
_____	_____	Total Score

Well, not necessarily. It depends on which considerations are most important to you. If an increase in travel will ruin your marriage, then it won't matter how many positive considerations point to the new job. (This is assuming you want to stay married.)

However, a simple tallying of the score can be very helpful when the decision is a tough one, and no single consideration acts as a "knockout" factor. Besides, mathematical "logic" can be used to justify what you already feel to be the right decision.

The economic factor

Compensation, of course, will be a key factor in your decision whether to accept a new position.

Oddly, few people take time to really understand their economic choices, mostly because there are many hidden factors, such as cost of living, benefits, relocation expenses and so forth.

Regardless of where compensation ranks on your list of priorities, it's a good idea to know what you may be getting into when faced with a career decision.

To help you put your economic choices into perspective, use the compensation comparison on the next page to evaluate both your prospective compensation package and what you're currently earning.

The best time to make your calculations is before an offer is made. That way, you can form a clear idea of what you'll need, without having to haggle (or experience shock) later on.

If you're looking at an opportunity that's in a different geographic location, you might want to do some investigating before you even interview. For example, if you live in a nice suburban neighborhood in Lawrence, Kan., what would it cost you to maintain your current lifestyle in an area like San Francisco? Your answer (and your willingness to make the necessary trade-offs) will help determine your level of interest when considering the new position.

Bottom lines and porcupines

Regardless of who you're dealing with at the company (or if you're working through a headhunter), the best approach to

171

Annual Compensation
Where do you stand?

Current Job

Base salary $_____

Bonus, perks $_____

Profit sharing $_____

Pension $_____

401(k) contribution, tax savings $_____

(subtract) Non-reimbursed expenses $_____

Total $_____

New Job

Base salary $_____

Bonus, perks $_____

Profit sharing $_____

Pension $_____

401(k) contribution, tax savings $_____

(subtract) Non-reimbursed expenses $_____

(add or subtract) Cost of living differential $_____

(subtract) Non-reimbursed moving expenses $_____

(subtract) Additional tax liability $_____

Total $_____

putting the deal together is to decide whether you want the job *before* an offer is extended. This allows you to clarify whether the job suits your needs. Unless you're motivated solely by money, it's doubtful a few extra dollars will turn a bad job into a good one.

If the job interests you, then determine the conditions under which you'll accept. These fall into two categories: *bottom lines* and *porcupines.*

The term bottom line refers to the amount of compensation you feel is absolutely necessary to accept the job offer. If, for example, you really *want* $46,000 but would *think about* $45,000, then you haven't established your bottom line. The bottom line is one dollar more than the figure you would positively walk away from. Setting a bottom line clarifies your sense of worth, and helps avoid an unpredictable bargaining session.

I recommend against "negotiating" an offer in the classic sense, where the company makes a proposal, you counter it, they counter your counter, and so on. While this type of *tit for tat* format may be customary for negotiating a residential real estate deal, job offers should be handled in a more straightforward manner.

Here's how: Determine your bottom line in advance, and wait for the offer. If the company offers you more than your bottom line, great. If they offer you less, then you have the option of turning the offer down or revealing to them your bottom line as a condition of acceptance. At that point, they can raise the ante or walk away.

Or, if before the offer is made, the company makes an inquiry as to what it would take for you to come aboard, level with them. Give them your bottom line, and suggest that they come in a little above the number you give, as an act of good faith. Be sure to let them know that you have no intention of dickering; if they try to *lowball* you by offering less than your minimum, the deal is off.

Put your cards on the table

A big part of my job as a headhunter is to put together two interested parties. Over the years, I've used the *bottom-line close,* a technique designed to help me discover a candidate's bottom line before an offer is extended. Once the bottom line is known, we can usually avoid the haggling that so often causes aggravation, disappointment or hurt feelings.

As I mentioned before, it's much better to put your cards on the table in the beginning than to have to barter to get what you want. An employer can get very irritable when a candidate says, "I'll think it over," or keeps coming back with new demands again and again. Even if you get what you want, you've created a negative impression with the company, which will carry over after you've been hired. In effect, you may win the battle, but lose the war.

By determining your own acceptance conditions in advance, you'll never be accused of negotiating in bad faith or of being indecisive. Whether you're representing yourself or working with a recruiter, learning to differentiate between financial fact and fantasy will facilitate the job-changing process.

In the following dialogue, notice how the recruiter zeros in on the bottom line:

Recruiter: *(To the candidate)* Well, Barbara, from what you've told me, the job with my client company is just right for you. Now all I need to know is how much it would take for you to accept the position, should they make you an offer.

Candidate: Bill, I've given it a lot of thought, and I've decided that I'm going to need at least $45,000 to start.

Recruiter: All right, so if they offer you $45,000, I can accept on your behalf, and you'll resign your current position and start in two weeks.

Candidate: Right.

Recruiter: Barbara, let me understand what you're saying. If I can't get you $45,000, but can only get you $44,000, I should tell them you're not interested.

Candidate: No, I'd have to think about it.

Recruiter: Gee, I wish we had the luxury to let you think it over, but I'm obligated to my client only to extend an offer that will be accepted.

Candidate: Hey, whose side are you on?

Recruiter: My job is to put good people and good companies together, not keep them apart. What you earn for a living is *your* business. I'll try to get you as much as I can, but I need to know what you'll accept, so no one's feelings will be hurt.

Candidate: Well, I guess I could live with $44,000.

Recruiter: So I can accept $44,000 on your behalf.

Candidate: Correct.

Recruiter: So if they can't offer you $44,000, but can only offer you $43,000, I should tell them you're not interested.

Candidate: Exactly. I would turn down an offer of $43,000.

Recruiter: All right. I'll work to get you the highest salary I can, but just so we're clear, if they offer you $44,000, I can accept the offer on your behalf, and you'll start in two weeks.

Candidate: Yes.

Recruiter: One last thing. Let's suppose that in good faith, the company, for whatever reason, can only offer you the $44,000 you said you'd accept. Are you going to be happy working for them?

Candidate: Well, I'd like to make as much as possible; you can understand that. But to answer your question; yes, I'd be happy with that.

Recruiter: Good, Barbara. I'll call you as soon as I talk to my client.

Notice how the recruiter "closed" the candidate on accepting $44,000? Now, if the company offers less money, the recruiter knows exactly what it's going to take to put the deal together, without second-guessing the candidate, or initiating an unpredictable negotiation.

175

If you're representing yourself, think: *What would it take to accept the job, should the company make me an offer? What amount of money is the break point, the point at which I'd walk away, when considering all the factors?*

You may want to itemize your bottom line, and, if it's appropriate, show it to the company as a means to justify your salary request. Carefully figure your total package, and document any loss of income that may result from a differential in benefits, geographic location, car expenses and the like.

The bottom-line close isn't meant to manipulate or lowball candidates; it's simply a technique I use to help people clarify their thoughts about money.

The porcupine close

Of course, there are considerations aside from money that usually need to be satisfied before an offer can be accepted. Factors such as your new position title, review periods, work schedule, vacation allotment and promotion opportunities are important, and should be looked at carefully.

To understand the candidate's needs, I use the *porcupine close* to quantify each consideration or "point" made by the candidate as a condition for acceptance. Once I close on each point, I can work with the company to put the deal together, without having to go back later to get "one more thing."

The following is a dialogue with a candidate in which I use the porcupine close. Try this technique on yourself, just to see what conditions must be met.

Recruiter: *(To the candidate)* Barbara, from what you tell me, my client's position looks perfect to you; so perfect, in fact, that you've authorized me to accept any offer over $44,000. Do you have any other questions or concerns?

Candidate: One little thing. I've already booked a flight back to Utah for next June. My brother is getting married, and I need to take that week off to attend the wedding.

Recruiter: All right, so before I accept this position for you, we have to make sure that you can take that trip. Anything else?

Candidate: I'm not completely clear on the new company's medical benefits. Do you know anything about them?

Recruiter: I know they're fairly standard in the industry, and should be comparable to what you have now. Let me double-check that, but should I go ahead and accept the job if they are?

Candidate: Sure, that would be fine. One more thing. My present company is paying for my tuition at night school. Do you think the new company can also do that for me?

Recruiter: I'm not sure. Are your studies at night school related to your work?

Candidate: Oh, absolutely. In fact, my night school class helped me earn my ASQC certification.

Recruiter: Well, then, Barbara, I'll see what I can do. If I can't get you the night school tuition, does that mean you won't accept their offer?

Candidate: No, but it would be a nice fringe benefit.

Recruiter: All right. Anything else?

Candidate: Well, I'm a little embarrassed to bring this up...

Recruiter: It's OK, you can tell me.

Candidate: You see, when my husband and I got divorced, I got custody of our pet poodle, Thor.

Recruiter: Thor?

Candidate: Yes. And Thor was simply *devastated* by the separation.

Recruiter: Oh, how terrible.

Candidate: To ease the trauma, Thor has an appointment with a canine therapist every Wednesday morning at 8.

So every Wednesday morning, I'm going to be a little late to work. Naturally, I'll make up the lost time later in the day.

Recruiter: You'd like me to get the company to go along with that?

Candidate: Yes. That would have to be a stipulation for my accepting any offer.

Recruiter: All right, I'll see what I can do. Anything else?

Candidate: No, that's it.

Recruiter: You're sure?

Candidate: Yes, positive.

Recruiter: Then let me summarize. I can accept the offer on your behalf if the company comes up with at least $44,000 in annual starting salary.

In addition, you'll need a week off next June to attend your brother's wedding in Utah. I'll check on their medical benefits and make sure they're comparable to what you have now. I'll also see if I can get you tuition reimbursement for your night school studies, which are directly related to your work, but that's optional, not mandatory. And we'll have to get the company to allow you to arrive late every Wednesday morning, so you can take Thor, your poodle, to his therapist; otherwise, the deal's off.

If I can get you those things, along with the salary we discussed, you'll accept the job and start in two weeks, right?

Candidate: Right.

Recruiter: Did I leave anything out, or is there anything you'd like to add?

Candidate: No, that's it.

Recruiter: OK, Barbara, I'll call you as soon as I talk to the company.

Once you know your bottom line, and each condition, or point on the porcupine, you're in a better position to get what you want, since you've established quantifiable goals to shoot for.

How an offer is staged

Every company makes hiring decisions differently. Some will encourage shoot-from-the-hip managers to make job offers on the spot. Other companies will limit the decision-maker's ability to act quickly and unilaterally, and require a drawn-out series of staff meetings, subsequent interviews, corporate signatures, and so on.

These days, it's not uncommon for the hiring cycle to last weeks or even months, regardless of how "critical" the position might be. The best approach is to maintain contact with the company, allowing for the fact that there'll probably be some delay. Presumably, you asked what the hiring procedure was when you first interviewed. Their answer should give you some indication as to when a decision will be made.

Offers can be extended by either a letter, or verbally from a hiring manager. They can also be made through a third party, such as a recruiter. In either case, be careful. An offer needs to include these three components before it can be considered official:

1. Your *position title.*

2. Your *starting salary.*

3. Your *start date.*

Before you resign from your present job, make sure you nail down each of these components from a company official, either verbally or in writing (in the form of an offer letter). Even if the offer comes through a headhunter, you should always contact the employer directly, and if possible, get a letter of offer or acceptance to verify the deal (although a verbal offer and acceptance will act as a legal contract).

Not long ago, I was working with a candidate who interviewed for a position with one of my client companies. The interview went extremely well; so well that the vice president of the company called the candidate at his home that evening to discuss the offer.

"Well, Paul, we really like you," the employer told the candidate. "The job is yours if you want it."

"I want it," said Paul. "When do I start?"

"Well, I'll call Bill tomorrow and work out the details," replied the employer.

Understandably, Paul got excited. Filled with pride, he drove his ailing grandmother by the new company the next day, so he could show off his new place of work.

But guess what? The employer never called me, and never called Paul, either. For some reason he changed his mind, and didn't have the decency to let anyone know.

The reason I tell this story is to warn you that even when the cat seems to be in the bag, it ain't over 'til the fat lady sings. An offer has to include a position title, a starting salary and a start date to be official; just telling you the job is yours isn't enough.

Here's another word of caution: Offers sometimes have strings, or *contingencies,* attached. Don't be surprised if the fine print requires you to:

- Pass a physical examination.
- Document your citizenship or immigration status.
- Obtain a security clearance.
- Undergo a thorough background investigation, in which your credit history, police records and travel history might be examined.
- Verify your academic credentials.
- Provide proof of your past employment, salary or military service.

Very often, these contingencies must be satisfied before you can to report to work or receive a paycheck.

Close it on your own

Waiting for an offer to be extended can often be a frustrating experience. If you find your patience running thin, here's a technique to speed things up.

Assuming there's mutual interest, but you feel the employer is dragging his or her feet, use the following script:

"Mr. Employer, this job looks very good to me. Can you think of any reason why we can't just put this together right now and have me start to work in two weeks?"

Based on the response, you'll either get the job immediately, or find out what's standing in the way.

Accepting the offer

If everything about the new position is satisfactory, go ahead and accept the offer. If you're expecting an offer from a second company, you should let the second company know about your offer right away, so they can speed up their decision. That way, you'll avoid jeopardizing one deal for the sake of another.

Once an offer's on the table, it makes common sense to accept or reject it within a day or so. Otherwise, your inability to commit will reflect poorly on the way you make decisions; or it will telegraph your lack of enthusiasm to the new employer. In either case, you're likely to be bruised by waiting too long.

If you have legitimate concerns, or you still have questions that need to be answered, now is the time to bring them up. Rather than tell the employer, "I'll have to think it over," use the following script:

"Mr. Employer, this job looks very good to me, and I'm enthusiastic about coming to work for your company. I'll be in a position to accept your offer and start in two weeks if I can just clarify a couple of things..."

The answers you get will make your decision for you, and you'll either accept or reject the company's offer.

If you decide to reject an offer, remember that it's almost impossible to resurrect the deal at a later date, since the position will be offered to someone else, or the employer will feel insulted, and close the door on your candidacy. Whatever you do, make certain your decision is final.

New angles and weird deals

Most deals come together quite cleanly, with little need for haggling or creative financing. Sometimes, though, it takes a little imagination to satisfy both parties.

Money can present a problem for employers when your salary requirements exceed the published range for the position, or create an inequity within the department. In fact, *salary equity* issues (in which your expected salary might be greater than someone on the staff who has more professional seniority) are the cause of most deals that fail to close for financial reasons.

To satisfy money matters, look for ways to increase your *overall yearly compensation,* rather than your *annual salary.* Here are a few added goodies you can shoot for to boost your earnings without ruffling too many feathers:

- A **sign-on bonus** to be paid in cash on your date of start.
- A **performance bonus** to be paid after 30, 60 or 90 days, assuming your clearly defined goals are met.
- A **discretionary bonus** to be paid in a lump sum, or over a specified period.
- A generous **relocation bonus** to be paid on your date of start to cover expenses (but which can be spent at your discretion).
- An **accelerated review,** which would occur after three or six months, rather than on your first anniversary of employment, in which your salary would be increased.

- An **early participation** in the company's bonus, stock purchase, or pension plan; or other employee benefit program.

When required, companies will sometimes serve up these tasty morsels to hungry candidates who recognize that overall compensation consists of more than salary alone.

The craziest deal I ever put together involved a candidate who'd just purchased a home and was beyond commuting distance to the interested company. Since the candidate wouldn't sell his home and relocate, the company president agreed to lease the candidate (who had a pilot's license) a single-engine airplane so he could *fly* to work each day. It just goes to show, where there's a will, there's a way.

> *With creativity as a tool, you can often close the "impossible" deal.*

12 Your New Job: Making a Smooth Transition

Congratulations! You've accepted a new job.

Now, take a deep breath and prepare yourself for the challenge ahead. Even though you may be floating on cloud nine now, there are a lot of emotional and logistical hurdles yet to clear.

As we discussed in Chapter 2, the job-changing process arouses all sorts of feelings. During the transitional phase that begins with your acceptance of an offer and ends a month or two after you've started your new position, the *emotional limbo* you'll experience will be especially acute.

Why? Because suddenly, the reality kicks in. After all this time, the changes you've been contemplating are actually happening.

This jolting realization will be followed by a sense of guilt. *Oh, my God,* you tell yourself. *I've been cheating on my present employer. Having an affair is one thing—but divorce? I never knew it would come to this!*

Then the fear of reprisal begins. *My boss is gonna kill me, I just know it. He's really gonna make me suffer.*

And if the fear of guilt and reprisal don't give you enough to worry about, consider the buyer's remorse you'll probably feel. *What if I made a mistake?* you ask yourself. *I'm gonna ruin my life. Aaauuuggghhh!*

Don't let the demons get you down

Relax. Everyone who changes jobs is plagued by these demons, to a greater or lesser degree. It's only natural. But rather than dwell on the past, imagine for a moment that you're in your new job.

> *Isn't this great? Think of all the changes I'm making, and how my new life is a huge improvement compared to what I had before. Think of the new people I'm meeting, the new skills I'm acquiring, and the new opportunities I have to advance my career.*
>
> *Now, am I going to let my fears unravel everything I've accomplished in the way of self-evaluation, planning, resume writing, interviewing and putting a deal together? No way! I'm not the type of person who's going to allow cold feet to put the chill on changing jobs. I'm a person of action, and I seize the moment. I know that those who back away from golden opportunities may never get another chance.*

Self-affirmations like these can do wonders for maintaining your positive energy and high self-esteem. And by projecting all the beneficial aspects of your new job into the present tense, you'll ward off the demons that can distort your judgment, and make you vulnerable to a counteroffer attempt.

Considering the counteroffer

Of course, if your motivation for getting a job offer was to position yourself for a counteroffer, then you're in the catbird's seat—you can't lose either way.

Or can you? Some employment experts point out that accepting a counteroffer is the equivalent of career suicide.

According to Paul Hawkinson, publisher of *The Fordyce Letter*, your acceptance of a counteroffer could very well blow up in your face.

Here's how. Let's say you announce your plans to leave your current job. This, in effect, blackmails your boss, who makes you a counteroffer only to keep you until he can find your replacement, at which point you're dropped like a hot potato. In the meantime, the trusting relationship you've enjoyed with your current supervisors and peers abruptly ends, and your loyalty becomes forever suspect.

Is this sort of scenario accurate? I guess it depends. My experience has been mixed. That is, some of the candidates I've known who've accepted counteroffers have remained at their old jobs for *years*, and have smoothed over whatever difficulties caused their split in the first place.

It's precisely for this reason that I'm so cautious when I work with currently employed job seekers. I want to feel confident that their motives are pure before we both invest a lot of time and energy in testing the market.

However, there's a lot of evidence to support the theory that candidates who accept counteroffers become damaged goods once they've been herded back into the fold.

Here come the three stages

If your intention to make a change is sincere, and a counteroffer by your current company won't change your decision to leave, you should still keep up your guard. A counteroffer attempt can be potentially devastating, both on a personal and professional level. Unless you know how to diffuse your current employer's retaliation against your resignation, you may end up psychologically wounded, or right back at the job you wanted to leave.

The best way to shield yourself from the inevitable mixture of emotions surrounding the act of submitting your resignation is to remember that employers follow a predictable, three-stage pattern when faced with a resignation:

1. They'll be in *shock.* "You sure picked a fine time to leave! Who's going to finish the project?"

The implication is that you're irreplaceable. They might as well ask, "How will we ever get the work done without you?"

To answer this assertion, you can reply, "If I were run over by a truck on my way to work tomorrow, I feel that somehow this company would survive."

2. They'll start to *probe.* "Who's the new company? What sort of position did you accept? What are they paying you?"

Here you must be careful not to disclose too much information, or appear too enthusiastic. Otherwise, you run the risk of feeding your current employer with ammunition he can use against you later, such as, "I've heard some pretty terrible things about your new company" or, "They'll make everything look great until you actually get there. Then you'll see what a sweat shop that place really is."

3. They'll make you an *offer* to try and keep you from leaving. "You know that raise you and I were talking about a few months back? I forgot to tell you: We were just getting it processed yesterday."

To this you can respond, "Gee, today you seem pretty concerned about my happiness and well-being. Where were you yesterday, before I announced my intention to resign?"

It may take several days for the three stages to run their course, but believe me, sooner or later, you'll find yourself engaged in conversations similar to these.

More than once, candidates have called me after they've resigned, to tell me that their old company followed the three-stage pattern exactly as I described it. Not only were they prepared to diffuse the counteroffer attempt, they found the whole sequence to be almost comical in its predictability.

The proper way to resign

The first thing you need to consider is the timing of your resignation. Since two weeks' notice is considered the norm, make sure your resignation properly coincides with your start date at the new company.

You should always try to avoid an *extended* start date. Even if your new job begins in 10 weeks, don't give 10 weeks' notice; wait eight weeks and then give two weeks' notice. This way, you'll protect yourself from disaster, in the unlikely event your new company announces a hiring freeze a month before you come on board.

A Standard Letter of Resignation

June 4, 1993

Mr. Bruce Keir, VP Circulation
VIRGINIA BUSINESS
411 East Franklin St., Suite 105
Richmond, VA 23219

Dear Mr. Keir:

Saying good-bye to a friend is never easy.

However, I have accepted a new position with another company. My last day of employment with VIRGINIA BUSINESS will be Friday, June 18, 1993. My decision to leave VIRGINIA BUSINESS is final.

I appreciate all that you have done for me in the past, and hope that we can maintain a cordial, professional relationship in the future.

Sincerely,

David Nelson

David Nelson

cc: Goodloe Suttler, VP Human Resources

And by staying at your old job for only two weeks after you've announced your resignation, you won't be subjected to the envy, scorn or feelings of professional impotence that may result from your new role as a lame-duck employee.

Some companies will make your exit plans for you. I placed a candidate once whose employer had the security guard escort him out of the building the moment he announced his intention to go to work for a direct competitor. Fortunately, he was still given two weeks' pay.

Your resignation should be handled in person, preferably on a Friday afternoon. Ask your direct supervisor if you can speak with him privately in his office. When you announce your intention to resign, you should also hand your supervisor a letter that states your last date of employment with the company. Let him know that you've enjoyed working with him, but that an opportunity came along that you couldn't pass up, and that your decision to leave was made carefully, and doesn't reflect any negative feelings you have toward the company or the staff.

You should also add that your decision is final, and that you would prefer not to be made a counteroffer, since you wouldn't want your refusal to accept more money to appear as a personal affront.

Let your supervisor know that you appreciate all the company's done for you; and that you'll do everything in your power to make your departure as smooth and painless as possible.

Finally, ask if there's anything you can do during the transition period over the next two weeks, such as help train your successor, tie up loose ends, or delegate tasks.

Keep your resignation letter short, simple and to the point. There's no need to go into detail about your new job, or what led to your decision to leave. If these issues are important to your old employer, he'll schedule an *exit interview* for you, at which time you can hash out your differences *ad infinitum*.

Make sure to provide a photocopy of your resignation letter for your company's personnel file. This way, the circumstances surrounding your resignation will be well-documented for future reference.

In all likelihood, the human resources staff will want to meet with you to process your departure papers, or cover any questions you may have concerning the transfer of your medical insurance or retirement benefits.

Restrictive covenants

A growing number of companies, particularly in the high-tech fields, are beginning to bind their employees to non-compete agreements, either by implication or written contract. Such *restrictive covenants* represent an attempt by employers to prevent those people who have access to proprietary information from transferring trade secrets to direct competitors by any means, including employment.

As you can imagine, the expression "trade secrets" has about as many interpretations as the term "family values." Depending on your point of view (and what's at stake), a trade secret can be anything from an innovative scientific breakthrough in genetic engineering to knowing the combination of your locker at the company health club.

Non-compete agreements vary considerably in the restrictions they seek to impose, but usually they revolve around the issues of length of time, geographic location and industry affiliation. For example, if you work for a high-tech automotive electronics supplier in Detroit, your non-compete clause may prevent you from working for a similar company in the Detroit metropolitan area for a period of two years.

Although many of the non-compete claims that find their way into the courts are without merit, it's a good idea to carefully review any employment documents you may have signed since you started working for your present company. If you feel you might be vulnerable to a lawsuit or injunction, you can minimize your risk by taking the following precautions:

1. At the time of your resignation, be sure to surrender all company property in your possession, such as a company vehicle, office keys, ID badges, computer hardware and/or software, demonstration materials or credit cards.

2. Ask your supervisor to designate a *responsible company official* to oversee your exit, and to accompany you whenever you're "on site" in the future.

Since a non-compete clause (either valid or frivolous) can gum up your career, you might want to consult with an attorney before you resign. In any case, it's best to keep your bases covered.

Relocation specialists

Now that you've gotten your resignation out of the way, you need to shift your attention to the new company.

If a relocation is required, and you haven't done your house hunting, let me make a suggestion. Work with a relocation specialist, to give you a hand in finding a place to live in your new city or town.

Relocation specialists are brokers who make their living by matching candidates and *locations*, similar to the way recruiters match candidates and *employers*.

Relocation specialists will interview you and your spouse (or significant other). Once they discover your housing and lifestyle needs, they'll refer you to realtors who are familiar with the local communities that satisfy your needs. Relocation specialists receive a commission or *finder's fee* from the realtor, once a property is sold. There's no charge to you or your new employer.

Often, relocation specialists will be able to prequalify you for a mortgage loan, or refer you to an amenable mortgage broker or lending institution.

Relocation specialists can also be good at handling unusual situations. For example, a relocation specialist I was working with a few years ago was able to help a candidate's wife transfer her teaching credential from California to Michigan. Without the transfer, the candidate wouldn't have been able to accept my client company's offer.

In another instance, a relocation specialist was able to pinpoint the exact housing needs of a candidate and his wife, show them the perfect property, qualify them and arrange a 5-percent down mortgage loan with a bank—all in one morning.

That afternoon, the candidate went to his final interview with my client company and accepted their offer, secure in the knowledge that his relocation wouldn't be a problem.

If your new company has a relocation specialist on staff, fine. If not, ask for a recommendation. Your relocation is too important to leave to chance, or entrust to a randomly selected real estate agent. In the event you're unable to find an independent relocation specialist, you can probably hook up with a realtor who works mainly with executive corporate transfers. Century 21, for example, does an outstanding job of matching out-of-town buyers with desirable, local properties.

Culture shock and task clarity

At last, you've arrived! Welcome aboard.

In the beginning, your new job may seem overwhelming. After all, there are new people to meet, new systems to learn, new schedules to keep and new personalities to adjust to. In many ways, *culture shock* might be the best way to describe your first week.

The real key to early success with your new company boils down to the issue of *task clarity*. Task clarity refers not to your ability to do a certain job, but to your understanding of how the job's defined.

Task clarity is dependent upon the quality of communication between you and the person assigning the task. Any breakdown of task clarity will result in frustration or poor performance, or worse.

To illustrate, let me tell you the story of John, a technical writer I placed with a high-tech client company in California. Three weeks after John started in his new position, I called to ask him how everything was going.

"Fine," he answered. "They love me here. I've completed the documentation on everything they've assigned me."

Later that day, I placed a call to John's boss, expecting him to heap praise on me for my recruiting genius. Boy, was I in for a surprise!

"Bill, I'm afraid I have some bad news for you," said the manager. "I'm going to fire John this afternoon. It looks like we'll have to start the search all over again."

"Really?" I was stunned. "What seems to be the problem?"

"John hasn't produced any of the documentation we need for our customers, and we have to get the work done to meet our deadline. If John can't do the work, I'll have to find someone who can."

"That's odd," I said. "I talked to John this morning and he's under the impression that the documentation he's producing is exactly what you asked for. When was the last time the two of you sat down to discuss his assignment?"

"Oh gosh," replied the manager, "it must have been about three weeks ago, right after he started to work here."

"Well then, let me make a suggestion. The two of you should talk this through, because there's obviously been a communication breakdown. As far as John's concerned, he's doing a terrific job based on his perception of the assignment."

Changing jobs: A new beginning

A simple failure to communicate the task clearly in the beginning had almost resulted in John's termination three weeks after he started his new job. Fortunately, we were all able to dodge a bullet. After my call to the employer, John and his boss sat down to discuss the project. The assignment was quickly clarified, and John went on to complete the documentation needed to meet the deadline.

John was lucky that my intervention helped save his job. If you were placed by a headhunter, then make sure he keeps in touch with the company, to monitor your progress.

If you found the job on your own, you have a responsibility to sharpen and maintain your task clarity. Ask for a weekly review for the first month of your employment, and don't let things get set on *automatic pilot,* especially in the beginning.

> *Knowing what to expect will help you prepare for an enjoyable transition into your new job.*

13 Career Change, Unemployment, and Job Security

Every pocket billiard champion has one thing in common: The ability to plan ahead during the course of a match, and carefully set up a strategic sequence of shots. Naturally, it takes a certain amount of physical dexterity to properly handle a cue stick. But as anyone who's watched even a few games of eight-ball knows, the player who wins the game is usually the one who can visualize several shots in advance, and through the judicious use of aim, velocity and *English,* coax the cue ball to ricochet into just the right position to make each ensuing shot a total piece of cake.

And so it is with the game of careers.

Most people who find themselves unemployed or in dead-end jobs are skilled, intelligent and hard-working. But unfortunately, they've either misunderstood their current market position or have failed to effectively plan for the future. Somewhere along the way, they've neglected to set up their shots.

It's a sad fact that in the last decade of the 20th century, the job security known to our parents' generation has become a nostalgic relic of the past. Thousands of high-paying white-collar jobs are continually being eliminated, and won't ever return; at least, not in their present form, or soon enough to really help those who are finding themselves squeezed. And although none of us would like to wake up one morning to find ourselves clinging to a career rug that's being yanked from under our feet (like the rust-belt steelworkers of the late 1970s), few of us have the wherewithal to explore our options before it's too late.

Several times each week, I'm contacted by middle managers and senior executives who've lost their "secure" jobs with little or no warning. Most of them eventually find new employment in their fields. But all too many end up accepting low-skilled, low-paying service jobs (or are forced to start businesses of their own) in an effort to make ends meet.

Your career: Meteor or misfire?

In his startling and insightful book, *The Work of Nations*, U.S. Secretary of Labor Robert B. Reich defines a future economy in which people fall into one of three job categories:

1. The **routine producers**, such as assembly line workers, data-entry clerks and inspection supervisors, are those who perform repetitive, noncreative tasks. According to Reich, these types of jobs are in a state of decline (both in terms of numbers and wages), as routine tasks become increasingly automated or employers shift their venues to offshore locations where wages are lower.

2. The **in-person servers**, such as bank tellers, security guards, retail sales clerks, taxi drivers, secretaries and hospital attendants, are those people whose physical presence is a requirement of the job. This category is characterized by its dependency on the fortunes others; that is, if there are no people to serve, there are no in-person server jobs to be had. (Who can forget George Bush's horrific vision of an American work force made up entirely of pizza delivery people?)

3. The **symbolic analysts** represent the only true wealth producers of the future, and the only occupational population whose star is collectively rising. Symbolic analysts are the people who identify, solve or broker problems. Their value to society is more a

function of the quality, originality, speed or ingenuity they provide than the actual number of
hours they work at repetitive tasks or their ability to
cater to others in person. Their tasks include the
manipulations of ideas, words, sounds, finances,
legal arguments and technology. Movie producers,
speech writers, composers, stockbrokers, litigators
and research scientists are just a few of the players
on this emerging economic stage.

What makes Reich's paradigm so compelling is that the
future is already upon us. Now, I'm not advocating that you
plan your career according to a political economic theory. But
in light of current trends, it might behoove you to take a closer
look at your long-term choices.

For example, will the high-tech training in computer
science you received in college ultimately cast you in the role of
a symbolic analyst (software development engineer), an in-
person server (hardware support engineer), or a routine
producer (COBOL programmer)? The answer may mean the
difference between a meteoric and a mundane career.

Remember, your association with a particular industry
doesn't by itself guarantee job security—just ask the aerospace
and defense workers of the *Star Wars* era, whose careers were
rendered dead on arrival once the cold war ended. It's the
supply of specific skills you bring to the party that'll keep you
in demand.

Planting the seeds of change

According to Dr. Len Oseas, a psychology professor at the
University of Cincinnati, all career changers have two things in
common: First, they're happier as a result of their switch; and
secondly, they prepared for their change either consciously or
unconsciously, long before the change occurred.

Let's suppose you hate your desk job, but you have this
little *hobby*. It seems you've spent the last 10 years hand-
crafting intricate, scale-model wooden ships. At first, you gave
them away to your friends as gifts, but then, as your reputation spread, you found yourself besieged by model ship

connoisseurs all over the country, eager to purchase your creations.

Given this scenario, it's not inconceivable that your carving skill, love of model ships and eagerness to share the fruits of your labors with others might lead to a new career in the mail-order marketing of specialty wooden *objets d'art*.

On the other hand, if you quit your desk job cold-turkey in order to open a TV repair business and you know nothing about electronics, you might find the going pretty rough, even if you love watching TV and derive pleasure from helping other people.

The difference between the two endeavors has as much to do with preparation as it does with love. For no matter how much you might enjoy singing in the shower, it's unlikely you'll perform the national anthem at the next Super Bowl without some type of practical or professional training.

Realistic self-appraisal

Much of the conventional job-changing wisdom contained in popular self-help books tends to be so romanticized or whimsical as to be practically worthless (or dangerous, depending on how many mouths you have to feed). Particularly ubiquitous are the how-to manuals that focus mainly on qualitative issues such as, "What types of tasks give me the most satisfaction?" or, "What sort of work environment do I really enjoy?"

These are important questions, to be sure. But the underlying assumption is that there's a plethora of neatly packaged jobs out there in the marketplace ready to satisfy every need.

Folks, let's get real. The stereotypical success story of the 45-year-old housewife with three kids and two years of community college under her belt who lands a high-paying dream job as a corporate planning executive with Megabucks International, Inc. (as a result of the "organizing" and "scheduling" skills she mastered as a Boy Scout den mother) is pure fantasy, and hardly jibes with the truth of today's employment marketplace. Any *realistic* career self-appraisal would have to probe for honest answers to the following questions:

- What specific training do I lack that's preventing me from getting the job I want?

- What type of obvious, quantifiable or highly special-ized training do I already have that will make me valuable to a particular employer?
- Is the training I need available to me at this time? If not, when will it be, or what can I substitute for it?
- Will the skills acquired from my present and future career endeavors continue to increase my value in the marketplace? Or will I be stuck in the same rut a year from now?

I don't mean to pop anyone's balloon by underestimating the power of intangible qualities, such as "communication skills," "winning personality," or "independent thinking." They are often the critical difference between a "hire" and "no-hire" decision. But make no mistake: If you're applying for a job that requires specialized training and/or a college degree, vague qualifications such as "goal-oriented, highly motivated self-starter with good customer interface skills" probably won't cut the muster when competing against those who meet the job's academic or technical requirements.

The family of occupations

Your challenge as a job-seeker is to identify or, if need be, *develop* a set of core skills that are valuable, transferable and ever-expandable. Once these skills are defined, the trick is to learn to apply them within a *family of occupations*.

What do I mean? Well, for every core skill you possess, there's a job function within a related group of employers or industries to which the skill applies. For example, if you're a chemist working for a chemical company in the lab, the "first cousin" to your present job might be in sales, either for a chemical company, a medical products distributor or a chemical process equipment manufacturer. Another related career might be in the field of food product quality control, or in environmental engineering, or in OSHA administration.

Not long ago, I was approached by a job-seeker who works as a marketing manager for a greeting card company. He wanted to stay in his hometown, but there were no other local greeting card companies to work for.

It wasn't until we figured out that the greeting card business represented just one niche in the *social expressions* industry that his options began to materialize. Put into the perspective of a family of occupations, his greeting card experience qualified him for several different marketing positions, each of them with businesses selling products or services that are "first cousins" to greeting cards: promotional outerwear, gift baskets, awards and promotions, and singing telegrams, to name just a few.

A satisfying progression

The fundamentals of "career planning" have changed. Whereas a generation ago, a person could plot with reasonable certainty a linear job progression through the company ranks (i.e., draftsman to engineer to engineering manager to plant manager to general manager), today the sequence is less predictable. In the modern world of corporate volatility, starting at the bottom doesn't necessarily guarantee a steady rise to the top. Either by design or circumstance, more people than ever are shifting gears.

Contemporary career planning requires you to define your set of skills and then apply them to a potentially wide range of employment opportunities. The degree to which you acquire, develop and utilize your expertise and interests over time will ultimately determine your career succession.

Rick, for example, worked for eight years as an applications programmer/analyst specializing in telecommunications and banking. After considerable soul-searching, he left his programming job and started his own management consulting firm, which helps client companies reduce their telephone costs.

Rick capitalized on his in-depth technical knowledge of telecommunications service and equipment billing procedures in order to provide a much-needed service to companies unable to wade through their own phone bills (which have become so complex, only a consultant can make sense of them!). Rick really enjoys what he does, and his business is thriving.

To the previous generation of wage earners, a career choice such as Rick's would probably appear illogical, since he left a "perfectly good job" to start his own business in a "different" field. But all Rick did was plug his core set of skills into a new application.

"Oh, sure," you say. "But what about my friend who just lucked into a great job? It had nothing to do with his previous training. What sort of planning was involved there?"

My answer is, that's great for your friend. But how many of us are serendipitously tapped on the shoulder by a long-lost relative to run a fully funded, phenomenally successful start-up company? I'd rather plan for the future than wait around for a miracle to happen.

Confronting your own job obsolescence

It's easy to make the mistake of investing in a career that ultimately goes nowhere. I can speak from experience.

Back in the early 1980s, I was a hot-shot guitar player who packed my bags and moved to Hollywood to pursue my dream of breaking into the recording studio scene, playing on movie and television soundtracks.

The only problem was, the emergence of keyboard synthesizers and advanced music recording technology had already made me (and thousands of other musicians like me) an obsolete commodity. Forward-thinking composers and producers had discovered that they could just as easily operate computer-enhanced multi-track studios in their garages by themselves as hire several different musicians to play the parts.

Some musicians I knew adapted to the change by investing in expensive, state-of-the-art synthesizers, sequencers, MIDIs, signal processors, drum machines and other articles of the faith. That is, they put themselves in a position to function fluently in the new digital language of sound.

But many of the session players I used to idolize when I arrived in L.A. are now scattered to the four winds, working day jobs. Sadly, they were caught off guard by the relentless (and mercilessly objective) evolution in audio technology.

Fortunately, I hedged my bets along the way by earning a couple of college degrees. Even by the 1980s, it was obvious to me how much importance society placed on higher education. In fact, the hysteria surrounding the possession of a sheepskin has, if anything, intensified in recent years. I know personnel managers who simply throw away any resume on which a college degree is missing. Fair? No way! Reality? I'm afraid so.

My *aria* of career obsolescence and involuntary transformation is hardly unique; it's being sung in a million different workplaces every day. Who would've thought, for example, that computer programmers would ever face the challenge of job obsolescence, due to a new generation of user-friendly computer systems, capable of utilizing code-generating software? It's a scary trend, but one that needs to be reckoned with.

Accessory to the climb

The point is, in a rapidly changing world, we're all affected by demographic, economic, political, or technological forces beyond our control. I'm not suggesting you panic and apply to law school tomorrow (oops, another vestige of "job security"). I just believe that the wall that might be blocking your career probably has some handwriting on it.

Luckily, the fundamental job-changing techniques we've discussed in *Take This Job and Leave It* can be universally effective, regardless of your situation. Whether you're unemployed, changing careers, or simply looking for a new challenge in your present field, your ability to establish a network, construct a dynamite resume, master the art of interviewing and execute a smooth transition will help give you the edge in a competitive market.

Career satisfaction is such a precious commodity; yet it's available to anyone with the determination and courage to find it. I believe that each of us deserves a job we can be happy with, and that it's each person's right to feel fulfilled in his or her chosen profession.

Whatever the economic challenges we face as a nation, we'll be more productive and twice as competitive in the global economy if we all enjoy our work—and allow ourselves to have a little fun during the job-search process.

Best of luck, and happy job hunting!

14 Job-Changing Resources

Your single most valuable resource is easy to use and free of charge—your local public library. There you'll find a full range of industry directories, specialty magazines and electronic databases.

The library can be a tremendous asset if you know how to use it. For example, a recent search assignment required me to compile a list of all high-tech companies in the Southeastern region of the United States that manufactured a certain type of electromechanical component part.

Using the *Cassis* system, I ran a computer search of all patent abstracts by subject, date and location. In practically no time, I was able to identify and locate all companies that had filed for patent protection for similar products or product improvements.

In addition to the many services provided by the library, I've included a list of resources that should help you target the job you want.

To meet the ever-increasing demands of the job-changing market, look for new, innovative services to emerge. For example, if you're unemployed or enjoy occupational variety, you might want to consider a position as an *executive temporary*. There's something out there for everyone!

Electronic Resume Listing Services

Advantage, Inc.
616 Frederick Road
Baltimore, MD 21228
800-628-9685
Provides a database of job-seekers' resumes for subscribing employers. Fee: $30/six months.

Career Placement Registry, Inc.
302 Swann Avenue
Alexandria, VA 22301
800-368-3093
An electronic resume listing service. For job-seekers with 0-5 years experience.

Job Bank, USA
8000 Thomas Cresent Drive, Suite 850
Vienna, VA 22182
703-761-4290
Provides subscribing employers access to your background and skills.

kiNexus
640 N. LaSalle Street, Suite 560
Chicago, IL 60610
800-828-0422
Provides subscribing employers in the U.S. access to your background and skills (all disciplines). Annual fee is $20 for students, $30 for nonstudents.

Peterson's Connexion
P.O. Box 2123
Princeton, NJ 08543-2123
800-338-3282
$40 fee, renewable every six months.

Job Listings & Clipping Services

ADNET Online
5987 East 71st Street, Suite 206
Indianapolis, IN 46220
Attn.: Resume Database Administrator
800-543-9974
Provides professional, managerial, and technical job listings of subscribing companies. Available to subscribers of home PC networks such as Prodigy, CompuServe, GEnie, and America Online.

American Employment Weekly
Scott Publishing Company
1636 Crestwood Blvd.
South Bend, IN 46635
219-235-3570
Weekly clippings of national classified ads. Single issue price: $3; or $38 quarterly, $60 semi-annually, $90 yearly.

Career Maker's Search Report
P.O. Box 531
Bath, OH 44210
800-248-9615
Publishes a listing of job openings in engineering and manufacturing on the 1st and 15th of every month.

CEO Job Opportunities Update
2011 Eye Street NW, Suite 600
Washington, DC 20006
202-331-3828
Biweekly publication lists jobs in nonprofit organizations only.

Job Ads USA (Executive Telecom System, Inc.)
9595 Valparaiso Court
Indianapolis, IN 46268
800-421-8884
Database of job listings on the Human Resource Information Network.

National Ad Search
P.O. Box 2083
Milwaukee, WI 53201
800-351-1398
The most extensive clipping service of weekly classified ads from newspapers across the U.S. Subscription rate: $235 yearly; $145 semi-annually; $75 quarterly.

National Business Employment Weekly
420 Lexington Avenue, Suite 2040
New York, NY 10170
800-628-9320
Weekly publication containing *The Wall Street Journal* classified ads. Includes articles on job-search strategies, career development, etc. Subscription rate: $199/yearly.

Network News
227 Commerce Street
East Haven, CT 06512
203-467-8870
Job listings published by the Association of MBA Executives.

Opportunities in Public Affairs
1100 Connecticut Avenue NW, Suite 700
Washington, DC 20036
202-861-5885
Publication that provides government and political job listings in the Washington, D.C., area.

Search Bulletin
8300 Boone Blvd., Suite 500
Vienna, VA 22182
703-848-9220 Fax: 703-848-4586
Twice-monthly periodical providing sales, marketing, general management, accounting, financial and corporate planning job openings to subscribers.

Sports Careers
P.O. Box 10129
Phoenix, AZ 85064
800-776-7877
Lists job openings in the sports industry.

"Retail" Outplacement

Bernard Haldane Associates
105 West Fourth Street, Suite 900
Cincinnati, OH 45202
800-966-0442
More than 40 offices in the U.S.

R.L. Stevens & Associates
800 South Street
Waltham, MA 02154-1439
617-647-4888

Contingency Search Firms—Generalist

Dunhill Personnel System, Inc.
1000 Woodbury Road
Woodbury, NY 11797
516-364-8800

Express Personnel Services
6300 Northwest Expressway
Oklahoma City, OK 73132
800-652-6400

Management Recruiters International
1127 Euclid Avenue, Suite 1440
Cleveland OH 44115
216-696-1122
The largest franchise, with offices in most U.S. cities.

Olsten Corporation
1 Merrick Avenue
Westbury, NY 11590
516-832-8200

Romac & Associates
183 Middle Street
Portland, ME 04112
800-341-0263

Roth Young Personnel Services, Inc.
535 Fifth Avenue
New York, NY 10017
212-557-8181

Sanford Rose Associates
265 South Main Street
Akron, OH 44308
216-762-6211

Search West, Inc.
1888 Century Park East, Ste. 2050
Los Angeles, CA 90067
510-284-8888

Snelling Personnel Services
12801 N. Central Expressway, Suite 250
Dallas, TX 75243
214-363-8800

Contingency Search Firms—Specialist

Accountants on Call
Park 80 West, Plaza Two
Garden State Parkway at I-80
Saddle Brook, NJ 07662
201-843-0006

Adia Personnel Services
64 Willow Place
Menlo Park, CA 94025
800-343-2342
Clerical and office support.

Healthcare Recruiters
5420 LBJ Freeway, Suite 575
Dallas, TX 75240
214-770-2020

Office Mates 5
1127 Euclid Avenue, Suite 1440
Cleveland OH 44115
216-696-1122
Clerical and office support.

Robert Half International
2884 Sand Hill Road, Suite 200
Menlo Park, CA 94025
415-854-9700
Accounting and finance.

Sales Consultants
1127 Euclid Avenue, Suite 1440
Cleveland OH 44115
216-696-1122

Source EDP
P.O. Box 152250
Irving, TX 75015
214-717-5005
Data processing.

Source Finance
P.O. Box 152250
Irving, TX 75015
214-717-5005
Accounting and finance.

Retained Search Firms

Heidrick & Struggles
245 Park Avenue
New York, NY 10167
212-867-9876

Korn/Ferry International
237 Park Avenue
New York, NY 10017
212-687-1834

Russell Reynolds Associates, Inc.
200 Park Avenue
New York, NY 10167
212-351-2000

Spencer Stuart & Associates
55 East 52nd Street
New York, NY 10055
212-407-0200

Search Firm Networks—Generalist

Inter-City Personnel Associates
P.O. Box 2275
Appleton, WI 54913
414-739-7788

National Personnel Associates
150 Fountain NE
Grand Rapids, MI 49503
616-459-5861

Nationwide Interchange Service
P.O. Box 20389
Canton, OH 44701-0389
216-455-1433

Search Firm Networks—Specialist

EDP Resource Group, Inc.
5960 Fairview Road, Suite 415
Charlotte, NC 28210
704-554-1500

First Interview
5500 Interstate North Parkway, Suite 425
Atlanta, GA 30328
404-952-1058
Sales and Marketing.

IPR Group
8097-B Roswell Road
Atlanta, GA 30350
404-396-7500
Insurance.

National Association of Physician Recruiters
P.O. Box 150127
Altamonte Springs, FL 32715-0127
407-774-7880

National Banking Network
2628 Barrett Beach
Virginia Beach, VA 23452
804-463-5766

National Computer Associates
115 West State Street
Media, PA 19063
215-565-8880

National Environmental Network
2628 Barrett Beach
Virginia Beach, VA 23452
804-463-5766

National Insurance Recruiters Network
P.O. Box 7811
Marietta, GA 30065-7811
404-565-5213

National Retail Network
P.O. Box 187
Hicksville, NY 11801
516-433-7847

Sales Network, Inc.
P.O. Box 920
Bardstown, KY 40004
502-348-2199

Executive Search Directories

Directory of Executive Recruiters
Templeton Road
Fitzwilliam, NH 03447
603-585-2200
Kennedy Publications. Lists search firms by specialization, and as being either retained or contingency.

National Directory of Personnel Consultants
3133 Mount Vernon Avenue
Alexandria, VA 22305
703-684-0180
Published by the National Association of Personnel Consultants; lists search firms by specialization.

The Recruiting & Search Report
P.O. Box 9433
Panama City Beach, FL 32417
904-235-3733
Exhaustive and up-to-date listing of executive search firms by industry specialization.

Third-Party Specialists

American Business Lists
5711 South 86th Circle
Omaha, NE 68127
402-331-7169
List broker; lists available for rent or purchase.

Cooper Heller Research, Inc.
622 South 42nd Street
Philadelphia, PA 19104
215-823-5490
Infopreneur.

Finders
616 Frederick Road
Baltimore, MD 21228
800-628-9685
Direct-mail service for job-seekers.

National Job Campaigning Resource Center
7205 Thomas Drive, Suite E-6
Panama City Beach, FL 32408
904-235-3733
Sells lists of executive search firms by industry and/or discipline; publishes a newsletter for job-seekers.

Qualified List Corporation
135 Bedford Road
Armonk, NY 10504
800-533-3713
List broker; lists for rent or purchase on disks or labels.

Job Fair Organizers

Business People, Inc. (BPI)
2985 Multifoods Tower
33 South 6th Street
Minneapolis, MN 55402
612-370-0550
Engineering, computer programming, governmental service.

Career Expo
2367 Auburn Avenue
Cincinnati, OH 45219
513-721-3030
Engineering, data processing, affirmative action.

Lendman Associates
5500 Greenwich Road
Virginia Beach, VA 23462
800-288-2890
Engineering, data processing, sales and marketing.

National Career Centers (NCC)
1830 Owen Drive, Suite L
Fayetteville, NC 28304
919-483-0413
Generalist.

Professional Exchange
4176 South Plaza Trail
Virginia Beach, VA 23452
804-431-0550
Engineering, data processing.

Recourse Communications
334 Knight Street, P.O. Box 1040
Warwick, RI 02887
401-732-9850
Generalist.

Westech
4701 Patrick Henry Drive, Suite 1901
Santa Clara, CA 95054
408-970-8800
Engineering, data processing.

About the Author

Bill Radin began his career in executive search after receiving his master's degree from the University of Southern California.

As a specialist in the permanent placement of electrical engineers, Bill quickly established himself as a top-producing consultant, serving the needs of a wide range of client companies, including such multinational giants as TRW, NEC, Westinghouse, Eaton and Mobil Oil. Under his leadership as department manager and training director, Bill helped Search West, Inc., of Los Angeles and Management Recruiters of Cincinnati set individual and company billing records.

In 1989, he founded Radin Associates, a full-service training and development resource for executive search practitioners, managers and search firm owner/operators.

His highly acclaimed, best-selling books, *Billing Power! The Recruiter's Guide to Peak Performance,* and *The Recruiter's Almanac of Scripts, Rebuttals, and Closes*, have been sold in the United States and seven foreign countries; and his frequent guest columns have appeared in industry trade magazines, such as *Weighing and Measurement* and *Personnel Consultant.*

Currently active as an executive search practitioner, Bill resides in Cincinnati, Ohio, with his wife, Ruth, and stepdaughter, Randi.

Index